PENGUIN BOOKS

OUR CURRENCY, OUR COUNTRY

John Redwood was born in 1951 in Dover and educated at Kent College, Canterbury, and Magdalen and St Antony's Colleges, Oxford. He began his career as a university teacher at Oxford. He spent fourteen years as a merchant banker with Flemings and Rothschilds and four years as an industrialist, becoming chairman of a quoted company. Between 1983 and 1985 he was Head of the Prime Minister's Policy Unit. In 1987 he was elected to Parliament, and he spent six years as a Minister, rising to Cabinet level.

Since contesting the leadership of the Conservative Party in 1995, he has taken the argument about the single currency to the country and the business community, holding a televised debate with Roy Hattersley, the Warwick University debate with Sir Leon Brittan and the CBI Harrogate debate with Sir David Simon. He is a regular contributor to *The Times*, the *Today* programme and to various other newspapers on this subject.

OUR CURRENCY, OUR COUNTRY

The Dangers of European Monetary Union

John Redwood

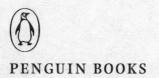

PENGUIN BOOKS

PENGUIN BOOKS

Published by the Penguin Group
Penguin Books Ltd, 27 Wrights Lane, London W8 5TZ, England
Penguin Books USA Inc., 375 Hudson Street, New York, New York 10014, USA
Penguin Books Australia Ltd, Ringwood, Victoria, Australia
Penguin Books Canada Ltd, 10 Alcorn Avenue, Toronto, Ontario, Canada M4V 3B2
Penguin Books (NZ) Ltd, 182–190 Wairau Road, Auckland 10, New Zealand

Penguin Books Ltd, Registered Offices: Harmondsworth, Middlesex, England

First published 1997
10 9 8 7 6 5 4 3 2 1

Grateful acknowledgement is given to the European Monetary Institute for
permission to reproduce tables.

Set in 10/13pt Monotype Photina
Typeset by Rowland Phototypesetting Ltd, Bury St Edmunds, Suffolk
Printed in England by Clays Ltd, St Ives plc

Contents

Preface

Europe is my continent, not my country. I want to help build a Europe which is more prosperous, which is democratic, which respects the different languages, cultures, religions and histories of the European peoples. We can do that by extending the Common Market eastwards, by encouraging more cooperation and agreement between governments and by supporting democratic institutions in each and every country.

Advocates of a single currency for a handful of countries in Western Europe make two main claims for it – peace and prosperity. To them it makes business and economic sense. They think it would save business the costs and uncertainties of exchange-rate movements. They look forward to a single-currency world of lower interest rates and faster growth. Yet the reality, when we all tried to prepare for it by pegging our currencies against each other, was higher interest rates, higher taxes, less growth and higher unemployment. However much the governments and central banks tried, the economies of Western Europe were not ready for currency union and the strains in the system became enormous.

For most British businesses it would be all cost and no benefit. They would have to change all their tills, slot and cash machines, but they have no DM or French-franc revenue to exchange.

Many supporters of the scheme see it as a much more fundamental issue than one of slower or faster growth. They see it as a matter of peace or war. They think that the single currency would be a major step on the road to a united Europe, where the disagreements and tensions between races, peoples, governments and religions would be a thing of the past. They want to abolish the risk of war between countries in Western Europe by abolishing the countries that have been to war with each other.

They look to the United States as an example of how it could work. But this is an unfortunate analogy: the USA was born of a war to throw off British rule, extended by a war against Mexico and finally united at the point of many a rifle in a murderous civil war between the states of the union. The USA was only one, the south was only won, when the uprising of the reluctant states was quelled by superior forces. I do not want a Europe like that, and see no reason to follow their example.

The single-currency scheme is already causing tensions and rows between countries in Western Europe, and between governments and their electorates. France wants a single currency without full political union as well. She wants to be able to exercise political control over and above the economic policy of the union. Germany wants political union alongside currency union: she effectively wants to merge the countries of Western Europe into one. Meanwhile she is strongly opposed to political or democratic control over money and the European Central Bank. Germany, Italy and Spain have been rowing over whether the Latin countries will be let in.

There have been riots on the streets of France against the spending cuts the currency scheme requires. Three quarters of the German people are opposed to the abolition of the DM, despite their government's insistence that it must go ahead. One in 8 Germans, 1 in 8 French people, 1 in 8 Italians, and almost 1 in 4 Spaniards are out of work. Despite that, their governments think that donning the single-currency hair shirt is more important than promoting growth and prosperity.

I want Britain to explain the damage this idea is now doing. We must remind Europe that the peace has been kept since 1945 by NATO, not by the European Community. We should remember that a peace-loving, democratic Germany is very different from the Germany of Hitler and that the balance of power has shifted decisively with the rise of the USA as the world's only superpower.

We should explain that we now live in a global market and a global world of fast communications. The idea of integrating between six and fifteen Western European countries is old-fashioned and backward looking. The danger is that Europe would become a backwater, cut off from the dynamic trade and investment opportunities of Asia, and isolated from the technical advances coming from both east and west.

You cannot have a single currency without a single interest rate, a single banking policy, a single budget and a single finance minister or Central Bank governor. You are led inevitably to a single taxation policy and a single economic policy. You are close to creating a single government.

Recent trends in Europe have been to create more countries and currencies, not fewer. If anything, the people of Europe want to live in smaller countries, not bigger. We have seen all the former Comecon countries replace the rouble with their own national money: they saw no advantage in a single common currency. No one can say the rouble made them rich. We have seen the Irish split away from the pound and set up their own punt. We have seen Yugoslavia fracture into many pieces.

A Europe of nations is the only Europe that can work. It must be a Europe of nations protected from threat by NATO, friends with the USA and Asia, open to the world, not closed to others. Europe's problem is not that it has too many currencies but that it has too few jobs.

PART 1
THE POLITICS

European integration does not stop wars

Europe has been war-torn since birth. Settled by different tribes over many centuries, several nations have tried to conquer and plunder the others. Imperial Rome, the barbarian hordes, the Islamic armies, the Spanish, the French and the Germans, the Austrians, the Russians and the Turks, have all had their ambitions. Sometimes these great powers have acted out of fear: fear for their own borders, fear that they are being encircled by others. Sometimes these powers have acted aggressively, believing that Europe would be better if it were more united under their direction. All these efforts at creating a European empire have failed, usually because a coalition of other states emerges which resists and ultimately overthrows the aggressor.

The most common argument for European integration – and therefore for the single currency – has been that going along with visions of a more integrated Western Europe would stop such wars ever happening again. This is reminiscent of the idealism at the end of the First World War, when many believed or wanted to believe that that had been the war to end all wars. We must ask ourselves if it is likely that strengthening a central government in Brussels and Frankfurt for up to fifteen countries in Western Europe can bring about that permanent peace which we would all like.

The presence of the European Community as a force on the world stage did not prevent war in Bosnia, on our borders. Indeed, the combined efforts of Community countries probably served to exacerbate and prolong that dreadful conflict, from the time when Germany and effectively the rest of us first recognized Croatia as a separate country to the time when the USA had to intervene to assist our overcommitted forces and impose some kind of settlement. As always with European matters this has caused a rift in interpretation. Some of us conclude from this sorry tale that NATO and the UN are the right international bodies to handle problems like this, and the intervention of the EU served only to complicate and worsen a bad position. Others deduce that we need a stronger EU with a European army at its command to intervene more extensively than the French and British armies did in Bosnia. The British army performed valiantly, but had to operate within ambiguous instructions from the UN and EC.

It is difficult to see how a stronger EU could prevent wars in the most unsettled parts of our continent. The war in the south of Russia goes on unaffected by European integration. Conflict is always possible in the East as the countries that have emerged from underneath the collapsing Soviet empire seek to establish their identities and fair boundaries. As the European Union regards strengthening central control as more important than widening the number of countries in its remit, it is expressly implying that creating a strong state in Western Europe is more important to it than trying to help stabilize the more unstable eastern part of Europe. The EU plan offers no hope of resolving the conflict between Greece and Turkey, no obvious solution to the question of how far the borders of the new Russia should stretch, no clear view on the relationship between Hungary and Romania or on the position east of the Elbe.

My main concern is with Britain. Our country has been involved in all too many European wars over the last two thousand years. We were conquered twice by continental aggression: first by the Romans, and then by the Normans. In the first millennium Danes and Norwegians raided and settled. Since 1066 we have recognized that we are a European country, by geography, history, interest and inclination. Although we have enjoyed obvious advantages from our island position, our history has been interwoven with that of the main continental countries.

There have been times when we have been the aggressor. After the Norman conquest of England, we repaid the compliment in some measure in the Middle Ages, when England asserted and often enforced territorial claims to parts of France, especially to Aquitaine and the Calais region; these were dropped in the sixteenth century and have never been revived. In the last five hundred years we have fought for colonies that other European countries claimed, in the interests of widening our commercial and territorial empire.

There is no likelihood of future wars based on British aggression. We do not seek new colonies or covet other people's territory. We now have largely settled frontiers, and have long since given up the idea that we ought to have more territory on the continent. No continental power has recently disputed our rights to the British Isles excluding the Republic of Ireland. There are no claims for the Isle of Wight or the Scillies. France accepts that the Channel Islands are crown territories, with a substantial amount of self-government, outside the EU. The only remaining issue between ourselves and a continental country over frontiers lies with our ownership of Gibraltar.

Spanish claims to Gibraltar often disrupt EU meetings. The EU has proved no more adept at resolving this dispute than the two disputants. As far as Britain is concerned Gibraltar is British, and should remain so. That is the wish of the people there, and it is ours by long practice. To say it is Spanish because it is close to Spain is as sensible as saying the Republic of Ireland is British because it is close to Britain and once was part of our union. This should not become a cause of war between Britain and Spain, with or without a European Union handling foreign policy. As long as the Gibraltarians want to remain British, and as long as we show resolve in wanting it to be British, the Spanish will realize that they cannot succeed diplomatically or militarily.

In the sixteenth and seventeenth centuries England stood against Spanish domination of the Low Countries and much else. Spain wished to impose a Catholic settlement on Anglican England and Presbyterian Scotland, as well as on Lutheran and Calvinistic communities in Holland and Belgium. An exclusive system of religion was to be forced on countries and peoples that favoured a more tolerant system, or a different style. England was critical in leading the resistance to such tyranny.

A more common cause of wars between the UK and some of her neighbours has been our wish to stop any single European country gaining hegemony over the continent. Britain has always felt her interests threatened if those parts of the continent closest to us fall under the control of one power. Napoleon showed us why this would be a terrible idea from the British point of view. He aimed at a continental system which excluded British goods and services from continental markets, ushering in a protectionist system orchestrated in the interests of France. Britain had to resist, and find coalition partners who would help take on the might of France.

In the twentieth century the UK, with the US, has twice had to stand firm against German domination of the continent. The Hitlerian scheme was for a Europe united under German influence or control, with a single European economy and currency to be imposed after a successful conclusion of the war. The mass genocide of the Jews and the scorn for democracy were but two of the many horrible features of these plans, which rightly led the Western democracies to fight.

The questions before us now are whether such an imperial scheme is likely to threaten us again and whether belonging to a deeper EU would prevent it. In this respect I am an optimist. I do not believe that the four large Western European continental countries harbour military and imperial ambitions any more. Of course Holland, Belgium, Denmark and Luxembourg have no intention of invading their far more powerful neighbours to establish themselves as the imperial power. Nor do I see any evidence that the new Spain or Italy are amassing forces or seeking to establish territorial claims over other parts of Europe.

If you press enthusiasts for a country called Europe to clarify how it might stop wars, they will often agree with what I have written so far. To them the advantage comes from ensuring that France and Germany will not go to war again. I find it surprising that they have so little confidence in democratic Germany and France that they think either might go to war with the other. I also find it difficult to understand how the Brussels institutions would stop them if they wished to do so.

While I do not think the current plans for European union are about to cause a war, I do think they are likely to cause greater tensions between countries and peoples in Western Europe than if we had no such plans. It is especially worrying that enthusiasts for union use the United States of America as their example. They argue that the common market of the USA needed a single currency and a single government to unite it and create its prosperity, and they say Europe by analogy needs the same.

History tells a different story. The USA was born from a war against Britain. It gained a sense of identity and community through the war of independence, throwing off British government control. It fought a war against Mexico to gain territory in the south. As the nineteenth century developed, so the great differences of style, attitude and social systems between the southern and northern states became more and more of a problem. The election of Lincoln, a northerner, as President, led directly to a bitter and bloody civil war. The issue was the power of the individual member states. The southern states claimed the right to secede from the union and conduct their own affairs. The northern states said they must not do so, but had to recognize the higher power of the federal institutions. The federal power won, because it was backed by the industrial and military might of the northern states. During the course of the conflict the issue of slavery became important, but it was comparatively late on that Lincoln declared against slavery for all the states. The prime, originating issue was the issue of state power against central control.

This is not a very prepossessing model for a United States of Europe. Europe has none of the advantages the USA had in its formation. The states of Western Europe do not have to unite to throw off some colonial power. The people migrating to the USA wanted something different: they disliked the countries and cultures they were leaving, and sought a better life. They were volunteering to become Americans. Most of us in Western Europe are not trying to leave behind our own cultures and identities, and are not looking to change the way in which we are governed. New arrivals in the USA were asked to swear allegiance and loyalty to the flag and the constitution of the USA. They were required to learn English, the common language, and were happy to accept the dollar, the common currency. Despite all these advantages compared to Western Europe, they entered a horrendous civil war before they could finally establish their federal destiny.

Would a deeper union make war between Germany and France impossible? No, it would not. It would make a future war different in kind: it would be about states' rights, or would take the form of an insurrection against the federal power, but it could still at root be a war between the French and German ways of doing things. The best guarantee of no more wars between France and Germany lies in both countries remaining prosperous democracies, where their governments and peoples will see no advantage in going to war. This has been the position since 1945, without a political union between the two countries. It also helps to have the USA, Britain and other well-armed allies interested in the peaceful future of Europe. NATO has kept the peace since the war. No Western European power has wanted to grab territory from a neighbour, but had it wanted to do so the NATO force would have been there to discourage it.

The argument that deeper political union would stop war pulls at the heartstrings. There is enough memory of the great wars for the peoples of Western Europe to fear another. But thought needs to be allied to the heartstrings, and thought tells you that political union would not stop future wars: only a community of interest between differing peoples, and/or enough force ranged on the side of peace can prevent future wars. Europe has proved this method works for more than fifty years.

The Franco-German relationship has become the crucial relationship in European politics. It is a strange relationship. For most of the postwar years France found leading the relationship easy. Germany was rehabilitating herself politically and, as a divided country, Western Germany alone was never disproportionately large. The merger of the two Germanies has changed all that fundamentally. Now France shows signs of schizophrenia and fear. On the one hand she throws her weight around by testing her nuclear weapons, reminding Germany and the rest of the world that she has an independent nuclear force and is more powerful militarily than Germany as a result. On the other hand, successive French leaders seem to take their orders or direction from Chancellor Kohl when it comes to the future of Europe. France struggles desperately to stay in the running for monetary and political union, whatever the cost in lost jobs and lost opportunities. She accepts the need to merge much of her country with Germany, as if Germany posed an immediate threat to her.

I remember asking a leading French politician once how she could believe that France would direct Germany and Europe, in the era after the Berlin Wall came down. She replied that she knew in her heart France could not, but could not think of an alternative to the policy they were following. French foreign policy is an accident waiting to happen. The French have traditionally been a proud and independent nation. They will not take kindly to their independence being squandered, if it does not bring many other benefits. French men and women have already taken to the streets in protest against the economic policies being followed in the name of monetary union.

Germany's attitude is becoming more bombastic. Since the wall came down and she was reunited, her centre of gravity has shifted eastwards, and her sense of her own power and influence has changed noticeably. Germany is a larger country than the other big three in Western Europe: France, the UK and Italy all have between 55 and 60 million people. The new Germany has 80 million. Although her living standards on average are now very similar to the other three countries, her total national output is around a third higher because of the higher population. The years of German engineering and manufacturing success and excellence in the 1970s and early 1980s have also left their legacy, with other European countries thinking Germany is stronger than she really is. Germany has the great advantage of being led by a man with a clear sense of direction, determined to pull Europe with him in the direction he wants. With France prepared to acquiesce in the German plan, with Britain undecided about the deeper union, and Italy finding it difficult to establish a stable government, Germany has a relatively easy task in asserting her view of European developments.

If the political union develops, the idea would be to create common defence forces and have a united foreign policy. What guarantee do we have that this would stop wars rather than create new ones? Presumably an armed European Union would take an interest in the conflicts of its members. Would such a union agree to take the Greek side in any argument with Turkey? Will the EU continue to favour Croatia against Serbia? How far might such a country go in asserting its view of how the whole Balkan area will be settled? What would the EU's view be in any border disputes affecting Poland, Hungary and Romania? Would the EU take the side of the Sudetenland Germans, who believe the lands they acquired in the 1930s in the Czech Republic and lost at the end of the war should be restored? How would the EU develop its relationship with Russia? Is it happy to allow Russia to do as she wishes in Chechnya? If Russia changed her policy towards Estonia, Latvia and Lithuania, would the EU object? If immigration from Algeria and other north African countries remains a problem for the Mediterranean areas of the EU, will the EU as a whole have to take a stronger line on these matters?

The EU of the fifteen has large and difficult borders. Beyond her borders lie a number of small, fragile, unstable countries. Can we be sure that an armed EU with a single foreign policy will help in each of these cases? Might not some of our neighbours find such a development alarming? Isn't it possible that Britain would get dragged into conflicts that might not otherwise trouble us?

The aim of the integrationists is to replace fifteen national foreign policies with a single one for the EU as a whole. In due course this would be done by majority voting: so far, it is done by unanimity or consensus. At the Inter-Governmental Conference proposals are being tabled to have a spokesman for the EU as a whole, with a full-time staff preparing a general foreign policy for the union. This would lead to more and more pressure being put on countries to conform to the general line, and to suppress their own national instincts or views. In due course it will need European forces to back it up.

This could again become a source of tension between member states, and a source of tension between individual member states and the union. Spain or Britain is going to be disappointed when union policy on who should control Gibraltar is decided. Greece is going to be disappointed if the union will not back her in all her arguments with Turkey. France will be unhappy if the attitude to Algeria is not the one she would like. Italy is concerned about the Balkans policy.

Monetary union has to be seen against this bigger political backdrop. It is part of the jigsaw of the new Europe: an important part, but only part of a huge plan to create a country called Europe. Those who regard it simply as an economic issue do a grave injustice to the vision of those who wish to bring it about. The idea behind currency union is to lock the economies of Western Europe into one. It began with the idea of the European Coal and Steel Community, bringing together the big industries that had fuelled the war machines of the main combatants in the first half of the century. It is now developing, with the idea of uniting the economies as a whole as one. It means one weapons industry, one steel and coal industry, one set of rules, one political purpose. A single economic policy would entail a major move towards one government. The ultimate aim is a single foreign and defence policy.

The argument that all this would mark an end to wars on our

continent is simply untrue. The presence of the enlarged EC trying to work together in foreign policy as elsewhere has not stopped wars in the 1990s in Europe. It has not stopped civil strife from the Irish nationalists, the Basque separatists or the African protesters in Paris. It has not stopped war in the Balkans or in the former Soviet empire. Britain has no territorial claims to enforce on the continent and no wish to embark on new colonial wars. It is very much in Britain's interest to keep the peace, and to keep the arteries of trade unclogged. It has not been in either France or Germany's interest to go to war in the second half of the twentieth century. There is no reason for them to do so in the future, and there is NATO and US power as the ultimate guarantors of the peace. Far from making war less likely, a stronger European Union could make disagreement and conflict, if not war, more likely. It adds another power to a complicated equation, before the issue of states' rights has been properly resolved.

2

Creating a country called Europe

The idea of monetary union is an important part of a far bigger whole. It is part of a plan to create a new country called Europe; part of the dream of a war-free, frontier-free area. It reveals the misunderstanding behind Britain's membership of the European Community. When we joined the EEC in 1973, Britain was assured by leading politicians that it was a trade arrangement. It was called the Common Market. In the government's White Paper it was made clear that Britain's sovereignty would not be damaged, that our legal system would remain the same and we would still be a parliamentary democracy.

All this was reinforced at the time of the referendum on British membership in 1975. We were told again that it was a trade arrangement, that it was essential for British jobs and prosperity, and that our main national interests and institutions would not be affected.

By 1992 the story had changed somewhat. A government paper issued to explain Maastricht to a British audience dealt explicitly with the question of those who felt cheated, who felt that a common market which they had joined was metamorphosing into a European state without their consent. The paper stated 'The original Community treaties aimed at an ever closer union amongst the peoples of Europe.' That is quite true, but that aspect of the Treaty of Rome did not hold centre stage in the case presented for joining or in the case presented for voting 'Yes' in the referendum campaign. The EEC was sold to the British people as a necessary way of protecting and extending their trade with the countries of Western Europe. Indeed it was implied we would lose trade or be blocked in some way from trading so freely with the rest of the EC if we did not join.

As the 1992 White Paper explained, Maastricht added new areas of EC authority to an already lengthy list. Some parts of education and health policy, vocational training, cultural policy, consumer protection, aid to developing countries, the development of trans-European networks and policies for industrial competitiveness were all added to a list which already encompassed agriculture, industry, trade, transport, budgetary policy, regional policy and much else besides.

The British government, conscious of the worry that the growing range of Community powers and actions was beginning to add up to an alternative government, stated clearly in 1992:

The Maastricht Treaty itself requires that the national identities of member states shall be respected. Fundamental areas of national life, such as the monarchy, the relationship between church and state, and the parliamentary system, cannot be touched by the Community. Getting the right balance between Community and national action is known as subsidiarity. It is now (for the first time) enshrined in the Maastricht Treaty ... The inclusion of this idea in the treaty marks a major change of direction in the Community.

The government clearly hoped that this would be true. However, the other members and European institutions saw Maastricht primarily as a treaty pushing forward European union, rather than reversing some of the powers already granted to European institutions by the Treaty of Rome and the Single European Act. The Treaty of Rome had expressed the aspiration of ever-closer union. The Single European Act had introduced more qualified majority voting to erode the power of veto over new policies, and now the Maastricht Treaty set out an overarching scheme of economic and monetary union, the ultimate end of the long economic journey begun in the 1950s with the Coal and Steel Community.

Successful states enjoy the loyalty and support of their citizens. People living within their boundaries accept the legitimacy of the state. They accept its institutions, and they feel they belong to it. In Western Europe a sense of nationhood has developed at different times in different regions, and is held with a different strength and intensity in different places. In some important countries it is very deep-rooted and goes back many centuries.

England has enjoyed a sense of nationhood and has accepted common governing institutions for more than a thousand years. France too developed its national pride early, with common institutions of government from Paris. The United Kingdom emerged in the sixteenth and seventeenth centuries. Holland fought for her independence in the sixteenth century and flourished as a state from the seventeenth century onwards. Denmark, Norway and Sweden experimented with a united Scandinavian kingdom, but decided that they were separate nations. The regions of Spain came together fighting off the Moors in the fifteenth century. Italy and Germany were products of nineteenth-century unification.

In each case there are some minorities within these nations who prefer to have two or more countries where currently one exists. Some Catalans and Basques would like independence from Spain. South and north Italy have never been entirely reconciled to one another's company. Irish Nationalists in Ulster would like Northern Ireland to become part of the Republic of Ireland. Although these are important matters to those battling over them, they are details compared with the larger picture. The bigger picture shows us millions of people all over Western Europe who feel strong loyalty to their nation and who are broadly happy with the pattern of national government, national languages and national institutions which they have inherited. In no case do people want fewer countries. In some cases people want more countries.

There have been several attempts at a wider pan-European unity. The most recent was the attempt of the Soviet Union to unite the eastern and central European countries in a common empire. They enjoyed a common market, a common means of settlement, a common defence and foreign policy. They were allowed to keep national governments, but these governments were very circumscribed in what they could do because their economies were controlled by the Comecon system and their foreign policies were dictated by Russian influence and a common army. They were prevented from having free elections in the Western style. This experiment lasted for more than forty years, but it could only be kept going by the use of force. Few wanted to leave Western Europe to settle in the new united East, although they were free to do so. Many wanted to leave the East and settle in the West; they were shot if they were detected trying to do so.

While it is true that the main defect of this attempt at union was the communist system which was imposed, it is also true that revolts against it were national, not pan-national popular uprisings. The collapse of communism came with a series of separate revolutions in different countries. The first cries of the rebels were not to change the economic system, but to restore their flags, cultures and identities. In some of the countries the communist party re-formed, still espousing the old policy of central planning, and continued to attract a substantial number of votes, but everyone seemed to want the resumption of their national identity.

Even where the states that had gone into the union were very small, as with Estonia, Latvia and Lithuania, they all wished to emerge with their own independence. It goes to prove that national loyalties go deep, and cannot be suppressed even after forty years of indoctrination. Even those who could not themselves remember a time when their country had had its own currency and its own army knew that those were things they wanted. In the one case where national identity did not immediately re-emerge, peoples sought to split up into even more states than had existed before the full communist takeover. The peoples of Yugoslavia rejected Yugoslavia as another artificial union, preferring Bosnia, Croatia and Serbia or even smaller regions, in which they felt a sense of linguistic, religious and national identity.

The nearest Europe has got to a voluntary union of more states came in the later Middle Ages with the Holy Roman Empire. Then there was a common language for the educated: Latin for works of scholarship, and court French for diplomacy and conversation. There was a common currency in the form of gold, used in trade according to the intrinsic value of the metal, whatever local or national symbols and suggestions of value might be stamped on it. There were some common governing institutions for the Low Countries and for much of central Europe. The territory was much expanded in the sixteenth century when Spain shared a monarch with the Empire. There was a common enemy – the hordes of Islam to the south – and a common belief in Catholic Christianity.

All this was shattered by the fears of France and by a series of nationalist revolts, often connected with the emergence of the Protestant religion. In England and Wales the official change to Protestantism was an act of government policy, to strengthen England's independence as a nation. The main aim was to throw off the power of the papal court and allow the king in Parliament to settle his own marriage and succession. Henry VIII was the first English Eurosceptic. In The Netherlands Protestantism was tied up with resentment at Spanish rule, while several German states also mixed their enthusiasm for throwing off the power of Rome with some scepticism about the value of imperial government.

The Austrian Hapsburg empire crumbled under the many religious and ethnic squabbles of the Balkans; the Roman empire fell to pieces when the legions lost their grip. Cultural, linguistic and local identity are more powerful and longer-lasting than any empire.

It is true that even a sense of identity can pass if it is not too strong, or if something much more powerful and appealing is offered, but this is rare. In my part of the UK people are happy to be both British and English. There is no yearning to go back to Wessex, which was once a strong kingdom. Yet in Wales, which became part of a British governing system five hundred years ago, there is still a strong sense of Welsh identity. Even though four out of five Welsh residents cannot speak the language, and even though a strong majority want to remain part of the UK, Welsh identity is still most important. Language is often the crucial issue; or else it is an ethnic or religious difference that matters. People do not feel strongly about Wessex, because Wessex feels a loyalty to the English language and the same Christian religion as England. Wales feels somewhat differently, because there is a loyalty to a different language. Bosnia feels very different from Serbia, because there are ethnic and religious differences.

Both Hitler and Napoleon sought to form a united continental Europe by war, diplomacy and alliances. Of course there is no comparison between some of the methods and means of these two great dictators, and the peaceful means to union of the present European project. None the less, we need to explain why their vision of European union was unacceptable to many people in Western Europe, and why they were unable to persuade people by diplomacy that theirs was the right approach. Again it was nationalism of a more local kind which upset their grand plans. Britain was able, in forming coalitions against Napoleon, to appeal to people's fears of their policies being dictated by France against their own local and national interest. In 1944–5 Britain and America were seen as liberators by most in France, even though France's government was collaborating with the Germans, and by many in Italy, even though their government had been a strong ally of Germany and had shared Germany's war aims. Fascism was no more able to appeal to pan-nationalism than communism was. These two evil tyrannies of the twentieth century were put down not just by force of arms, but by a sense of independence, freedom and national identity amongst the old nations of Europe.

Although things can and do change, and life can move on, we are all prisoners of history. It is most important to remind ourselves of the history when trying to answer the question whether a new European state could work. My answer is that it could not.

History shows that it should only be attempted by consent. It should be taken very slowly, if at all. It has to demonstrate major benefits over the present arrangements. People have to be reassured that their identities and interests are not being threatened by it. It has never worked in the past if based on force. It cannot work this time if it is based on withholding the truth from people. Abolish the pound and you abolish Britain. You make a decisive move towards a country called Europe governed from Brussels and Frankfurt.

One of the most worrying features of the argument in Britain has been the insistence by those who want more European integration that it has nothing to do with the creation of a single country or government. Yet reading the treaties and looking at the wide array of institutions already established in the name of the European Union shows that the intention *is* the establishment of a new country.

The Union is very keen to offer citizenship, and sees citizenship as a series of rights. A citizen of France or the United Kingdom has both rights and responsibilities. I know that the British government will come to my aid abroad if I have good cause. I know that a British passport will entitle me to enter most countries, and provides me with British embassy and consular support. I know that all British subjects have the right to a fair trial, the right to vote if they qualify on the electoral roll and the right to a wide range of public services. There are responsibilities as well. There is a duty to serve on juries if called, to serve in the armed forces in national emergencies, to pay taxes and obey the law.

The European concept of citizenship was clearly designed by public-relations minds: it appears to be all rights and no duties, but on closer examination it involves both. The European citizen now has the right to vote in European parliamentary elections and in local elections wherever he or she may be resident in the union. He or she has the right to travel throughout the union, showing only an identity card. The citizen can use the embassy and consular arrangements which the union is now establishing direct or through member states. The citizen can take a case to the European court.

The responsibilities on the other hand are indirect. The requirement to pay taxes is there, but the obligation is to pay them to the national authorities, who are then obliged to send them to the union authorities. Union armies are still in an embryo stage. There are some joint actions between the armies of member states, and now the formation of a Euro corps. Enlisting the troops is still a responsibility of the member state, but in more and more cases the armies are there to back up a common European foreign policy settled at union level.

The union buttresses its position with the citizenry from time to time by urging a 'people's Europe'. Its ideas have included easier travel, easier trade, more cultural and educational exchanges, more language learning and the single currency to facilitate shopping in different member states.

The concentration on presentation has led to the development of the flag and logo. The twelve stars symbol, yellow on a blue background, has become the recognized motif of the union. It is used universally in union documents and on union business. Whenever a grant of money is made for a project it is a term of the grant that a board carrying the flag is prominently displayed. The flag is used on every union occasion, and member states are encouraged to use it as well. Flags are usually national symbols. Free trade does not need flags; countries always have one. The twelve stars do not depict the member states, although there was a period during the development of the union when by coincidence there were both twelve members and twelve stars. The circle of stars is a Christian symbol: the Virgin Mary's halo. They remind us of the Catholic and Holy Roman Empire origins of the idea of European union. It is no coincidence that Charlemagne's name has been attached to one of the principal union buildings: he was a successful warrior emperor who extended imperial power in his day.

The European Union has an anthem, from Beethoven, which is used on occasions when national anthems would normally be played. The name union is itself an interesting recent development. The grouping we joined, colloquially known as the Common Market here in Britain, was officially the European Economic Community. Many on the continent and especially in Brussels used to drop the word 'economic' regularly from their description, showing an impatience with the Anglo-Saxon – and the treaty – view that this was only an economic or trading arrangement. The name was endorsed by the member states in the Treaty of Maastricht, when the EEC was officially renamed the European Community, and when a wider-ranging purpose was incorporated for the something called the European Union. The union is the European Community, with the addition of matters like foreign policy, immigration and border controls which are currently arranged between governments and not through official EC institutions. The intention is to blur this distinction, moving to a world where the European Court and majority voting will come to apply to foreign and home affairs as they do to much else already. At this point it is highly unlikely they will choose to call the expanded EC the European Community: it will be called the European Union.

Names, flags and anthems are symbols or indicators. Real power is exercised through law and institutions. The EC has its own supreme court, the European Court of Justice. This court models itself on the American Supreme Court, which was a crucial agent in expanding federal power in the nineteenth century in the USA. Sir Patrick Neill has charted how the ECJ has operated in the last thirty years to expand the remit of European law and above all to establish the supremacy of European law over national law. In a series of pioneering judgements the ECJ has now established to its own satisfaction and to the satisfaction of many others, including many national courts, its right to be the court of final appeal in a wide range of cases. Even more importantly, it is well on the way to establishing the principle that it can overturn any Act or decision of any member-state parliament, if it deems such an Act to be against the treaties.

The European Community is first and foremost a legal construction based on continental-style codes. The treaties themselves are expressed in looser and more straightforward language than much modern parliamentary legislation in Britain. At their worst they read like poor third-year translations from Latin. They combine very wide general statements of intent with specific measures and detailed provisions. The court nearly always looks to the general aim of European integration when coming to its decisions, and construes the treaties in the direction of more European power. There is plenty of scope to do so, given how wide-ranging the treaty is. The aims are set out in Article 2, as reported in the *Official Journal*:

The Community shall shave [*sic*] as its task, by establishing a common market and an economic and monetary union and by implementing the common policies or activities referred to in Article 3 and 3a, to promote throughout the Community a harmonious and balanced development of economic activities, sustainable and non-inflationary growth respecting the environment, a high degree of convergence of economic performance, a high level of employment and of social protection, the raising of the standard of living and quality of life, and economic and social cohesion and solidarity among member states.

The community's tasks, the treaty makes clear, are to be carried out by the institutions, the Parliament, the Council of Ministers, the Commission, the Court of Justice, the Court of Auditors and the European Bank. It is possible to interpret this system as something different from a superstate in the making, and many have chosen to do so. They say that the main decisions are still taken by the Council of Ministers, with each national government separately represented, and that some of the big issues are still settled by unanimous vote, so any state has a veto and can protect its own national interest. The Commission is there to help and carry out the wishes of the Council; the Parliament is still largely advisory; the court is needed to enforce decisions; the bank has yet to be created. Some say that the European Community or union is something different from a new country or state; that it is something more than a trading arrangement, it is a new concept.

None the less, it seems clear from the progress of the treaties, the changes of name and above all from the decisions being made by Commission and court that it is easiest to understand the union as a government in the making. A state claims allegiance from its citizens, it has a framework for their government, it develops policies in a wide range of areas. All this is true of the European Union. The intention is to create a United States of Europe, with a supreme court, a Parliament or Congress, and quite possibly in due course an elected rather than a selected president. The question before us is whether this could ever work successfully.

There are few examples in history or at the present time where peoples speaking different languages are happy to live in the same state. Language divides people. It is very difficult to have an effective democracy or accountable government if those governing cannot speak the language of some of those being governed. Misunderstandings and resentments build up. Different languages often also entail different ways of looking at the world and different customs.

Canada has shown how difficult it is to keep a bilingual democracy in being as a single country. Even though settlers went as volunteers to Canada many decades ago, and have been living side by side for generations, the French and English speakers find it difficult to agree that Canada should remain as a centralized, united, single country. The Province of Quebec has for some time been asserting itself; its representation abroad behaves more like a national government's representation than that of a province or state in a federal union. There has been persistent pressure from many Québecois either to govern more things for themselves, or to split altogether from the English-speaking provinces. It shows how deep-rooted these feelings are, when allied to a different language. Catalan separatism in Spain is connected with a different language. Irish independence was followed by a revival of Gaelic, with many official documents and letters offering some Gaelic as well as an English text. Most Welsh nationalists see the language as an important part of their identity, and a reason why Wales should be independently governed.

In Western Europe we are invited to believe that the eleven different national languages, to say nothing of the host of other languages and dialects, would not be a problem. The European

Community already finds working in so many different languages a strain on its translation systems. Very often the detailed working only takes places in two languages, French and English, and sometimes only a French text is available. This can be most frustrating for all those who are fluent in neither English nor French. There are occasions when the differences of meaning and tone are difficult to translate, leading to misunderstandings which were not intended by the parties. Many people in Western Europe speak, read and write only their own language. It is unlikely that Europe will be so different from other places which have found it so difficult to keep together a single state speaking different languages.

The United States was united around the English language. One of the entry requirements was a rudimentary grasp of the language; it was made clear to new migrants that they would be expected to live and work in English. The Republicans are now alarmed by the rise of Spanish speaking in the south, and are insisting on proper English education to reinforce the language as the cement of the union. In order to have a proper democratic debate, with common ideas and common disagreements, it is vital to have a single language.

The single currency, too, is part of this plan to create one country. One of the first steps the emerging countries of Eastern Europe each took when they were liberated from communism was to establish their own separate currencies. They did not think there were advantages in keeping the system of common settlement during the Comecon years in place. Similarly the Republic of Ireland, although a fellow member of the EC with Britain, decided in the 1970s to establish its own currency and to break from the pound. This was a further illustration, if one were needed, that nationhood matters and that currency is seen as an important part of nationhood.

It is not just a question of symbols, although they are potent. Over the centuries monarchs and emperors have had their images on the coin. Jesus said, 'Render unto Caesar what is Caesar's.' It is also a question of power. He who issues the banknotes can have a decisive influence on the state of the economy. As we will see in subsequent chapters, at the heart of the economic debates on the single currency lies the question of whether this economic power would be better or worse exercised by a central bank than by national banks and parliaments.

The project to create a new country is breathtaking in the scale of its ambition. It encompasses up to 350 million people in fifteen different countries. The intention is to establish a federal government covering most important policies. It is difficult to imagine how the architects believe such a body could ever be truly accountable to its citizens, how it would establish legitimacy. The German view is that there needs to be a stronger European Parliament. Gradually they see the Parliament gaining more power over the other Brussels institutions, although not over the central bank and economic policy. No one has ever propounded creating a proper elected Western European government to take over from the unelected Commission and from the indirectly elected Council of Ministers. The only way in which there could be democratic control would be through pan-European elections to a proper parliament, with the government being formed from the winning party or parties in the Parliament.

While the Germans would like to see the Parliament having a bigger say in passing new laws there is as yet no proposal for such a parliament to become a directly taxing body or for it to replace the Council of Ministers. Various countries propose a steady erosion of the individual veto in the council and the further accretion of powers to the Parliament, but all have so far fallen short of clarifying where power lies by decisively favouring the Parliament. Pan-European parties are gradually emerging through coalition and common platform between the two main groupings, the Christian Democrats and the socialists. There is an implicit assumption that coalition politics is more likely than the winner-takes-all, two-party model of Britain, and that the powers of the constitution will be more diffuse, less clearly focused on a democratic assembly than we would favour.

In the economic and monetary field the lack of democratic accountability is one of the most worrying features of the scheme. The European system of central banks, and especially the new EU Central Bank itself, at the heart of that system, are to be independent and extremely powerful. Their tasks are defined explicitly in the treaty: 'to define and implement the monetary policy of the Community; to conduct foreign exchange operations consistent with the provisions of Article 109 of this Treaty; to hold and manage the official foreign reserves of the member states; to promote the smooth operation of payments systems'. Article 107 of the treaty explains just how independent they are to be:

When exercising the powers and carrying out the tasks and duties conferred upon them by this treaty and the statute of the ESCB, neither the ECB, nor a national central bank, nor any member of their decision-making bodies shall seek or take instructions from Community institutions or bodies, from any government of a member state or from any other body. The Community institutions and bodies and the governments of the member states undertake to respect this principle and not to seek to influence the members of the decision-making bodies of the ECB or of the national central banks in the performance of their tasks.

The president, vice-president and the other members of the executive board of the European Bank, by treaty, have to be appointed for an eight-year term, which cannot be renewed. These provisions are a great bulwark to prevent any democratic influence at all over the monetary and currency policies being pursued by the European Bank.

Admirers of this scheme say that the very independence of the banks is vital to its success. It would be the triumph of technicians over politicians, of bankers over amateurs. The board has to be appointed 'from among persons of recognized standing and professional experience in monetary or banking matters by common accord of the governments of the member states at the level of heads of state or government, on a recommendation from the

Council, after it has consulted the European Parliament, and the governing council of the ECB'.

Exponents of it have in mind what they see as the great success of the German central bank in the post-Second-World-War era, which they believe has been based on the independence of that bank coupled with the pursuit of price stability as the prime aim. Certainly they have designed a European system based on those two presumptions. Article 105 says that 'the primary objective of ECB shall be to maintain price stability'. No other policy objective will be allowed to interfere with the aim of zero inflation.

It is true that in the period 1945–90 the German central bank had an excellent record for keeping inflation low compared to other Western countries. It did not, however, succeed in running the German economy with zero inflation or 'price stability'. I think we must assume that the treaty has in mind zero increases year on year in average prices as measured by a general index of prices, rather than wishing to freeze all prices. In advanced economies experiencing rapid technological change you should expect large changes in relative prices: computers, for example, have become progressively cheaper in recent years as more and more computing power has become available on microchips, while certain services heavily dependent on labour have become considerably dearer as wages and living standards have risen. These relative shifts in prices are wholly desirable, indeed vital to economic development.

The German experience in the 1945–90 period was heavily influenced by the German experience in the 1920s, when Germany had the worst inflation record in the West by a mile, and it wrecked her economy. German stamps and banknotes of the time were overprinted with extra noughts to try to keep up with the huge and rapid losses of value of the currency. The new Germany after the war naturally wanted a currency and a constitution that made such a development unlikely to happen again. The reason the central bank in Germany was able to pursue a lower inflation policy than her neighbours was primarily that there existed in Germany a political consensus in favour of doing so. It was a matter of cross-party agreement, of common political thought, that Germany needed an independent central bank committed to low inflation.

It was also the case in the postwar period that pursuing low inflation did not conflict with other aims of German economic policy. Germany experienced a long and sustained boom as she emerged from the rubble and ruins of the war. A ready supply of cheap labour from the East and a growing success in her education and training systems allowed her to rebuild Germany and create a strong economy based on the big industries of those days, engineering, steel and chemicals. The system worked. There was no need for the central bank to seek more permission or guidance from the politicians.

All this changed markedly when the Berlin Wall came down, and when Europe started to move to a single currency. The German Chancellor was desperate to reunite the two Germanies, even though the economy of the East was far behind the West in every way that mattered: wages were much lower; the supply and choice of consumer goods was very restricted; the factories were antiquated, labour practices poor and machinery exhausted. East Germany was in no position to compete with the West on equal terms. The central bank advised against a monetary union on terms favourable to Eastern Germany, pointing out that it would be inflationary. If the bank had been truly independent, as many think it was, that should have been an end to the matter.

Instead Chancellor Kohl ordered a currency and monetary union on terms very favourable to the East: twice as favourable as the bank thought advisable. The predictable happened. Far too many extra DMs were created to replace the Ostmark, which was peremptorily abolished. East German savers were happy they now had more of a currency which had some value. West Germans were horrified as the bills came in for rebuilding the East. People in the East understandably wanted the same levels of wages and benefits as the people in the West. Prices and wages soon escalated in East Germany as a rebuilding boom using federal money commenced and as all the extra DMs came into circulation. Germany ended up with higher inflation than Britain. It was also evident that Germany's central bank was not in fact independent; when the politicians wanted to meddle with monetary policy they could do so. The governor of the central bank who advised against merger resigned.

The lack of independence was proved again over the issue of European currency union. Before the Maastricht Treaty was agreed the German central bank advised that currency union with the rest of Western Europe was not in Germany's interest. The central bank thought that whatever the treaty might say about the conduct of monetary policy and the characteristics of the new currency, it would be influenced by the laxer monetary policies of the other member states. The central bank echoed the fears of many Germans that the new currency would be less strong, less inflation-proof than the DM. Germany, said the bank, should stay with her national currency, and return to the ways of relative prudence that had characterized her monetary policy up to 1990. Again the bank was overruled, and Germany became the decisive founder member of the scheme. It is true that the warnings of the bank and many German people influenced the German stance on the European Bank. It is because of German fears that the new currency will be weaker than the DM that a treaty has been signed which, if properly followed through, would create a currency considerably stronger than the DM.

No one believes that the new currency will be a zero-inflation currency, although that is required by the treaty and reinforced by the institutional architecture. Many market commentators and analysts believe that 'price stability' will be reinterpreted to mean 'low inflation' and that the system will settle for higher inflation than the German postwar average. I will return to that possibility. First it is important to examine the democratic consequences of implementing the treaty as drafted and signed.

Monetary policy is widely agreed to be central to determining levels of prices and employment of resources, especially labour.

Monetarist economists have concentrated on deducing from trends in the amount of money and credit in circulation the likely future levels of employment and prices. Their rivals, the Keynesians, look at somewhat different models of the economy, but in the work of their mentor, John Maynard Keynes, money has a starring part. Keynes himself believed that money growth and the levels of government deficits or surpluses had an important impact on the price and employment level. The signatories of the treaty wish to give sole control of money to the bank, and to control the level of deficits of member states in order to help the bank with its task of controlling the rate of money growth. This means that the most important aspects of economic policy will be taken out of the hands of the democratic process and given to a committee of experts.

Some say this would be a thoroughly good thing. They contrast the patchy record of economies where democratic politicians interfere with an ideal of a perfect economy run by well-intentioned and successful experts free from political interference. The only problem is, there is no example anywhere in the world of an economy made more successful by such a benign and independent form of regulation. In the postwar period many communists and fellow travellers argued that Eastern Europe and the Soviet Union had a great advantage through placing the economy in the hands of technocrats and central planners, free from democratic interference. The result of that experiment was mass poverty in the centrally planned economies; the highest living standards were found in the unruly, democratic USA.

Even if a case can be made for the independence of the bankers running monetary policy, we have to ask could it ever be sustained in countries which have a tradition of democracy and democratic expectations. The main issue in all postwar British elections has been the economy. At Bill Clinton's campaign headquarters in 1992, a poster reminded his supporters what the election was about: 'It's the economy, stupid.' In the world of the Maastricht Treaty, elections to the European Parliament and to Westminster would no longer be about the economy. By strict application of the treaty the Westminster government would be debarred from even trying to influence the conduct of economic policy, as would the European Parliament. Would people accept that?

If things went well it would have more chance of stability than if they did not. If, for example, a Europe with a single currency had unemployment of 2 per cent, no inflation, a growth rate of 3 per cent with reasonable expectations of that continuing and public spending growing by 2 per cent more than costs, then a political consensus would build around pursuing such a policy under the guidance of a powerful European Bank. Success could take the issue out of politics. My figures have not been chosen at random: my own constituency currently enjoys 2 per cent unemployment, and is probably growing at 3 per cent a year, while British public spending is budgeted to rise by 2 per cent more than prices this year and next. It shows that it can be achieved within Europe.

However, the situation the bank inherits is likely to be anything but that in much of Europe. Unemployment is 12 per cent in France and in Germany. Italy has 12.5 per cent unemployment, and if Spain joins she brings a massive 22 per cent. Growth is at a snail's pace. Each of those countries is being asked to cut public spending against the background of mass unemployment. It is difficult to believe they would say in such circumstances to their politicians, 'We are happy for you to take the issue of the economy out of politics.'

Some will say that while the bank will be very powerful over money and currency policy, there are still things member states' governments could do in response to the fears and worries of their electors if the system does not immediately deliver a land of milk and honey. The government, they say, would still have the power to settle public spending and tax rates. It could still offer grants and incentives to business or people. These claims also need dealing with.

It is true that under the treaty there is nothing to stop a member state following a policy of low spending and low taxation, or of high spending and high taxation. What it cannot do is to follow a neo-Keynesian policy of high deficits to stimulate growth and jobs. Nor can it devalue to make itself more competitive.

Some believe that a policy of low taxation stimulates industry and jobs. Indeed, all things being equal I would say that that is self-evidently true. A new firm setting up, or an old firm expanding in Europe, assuming other things were broadly the same, would far rather operate in the country where company tax was 25 per cent than where it was 50 per cent; would far rather earn salaries where the top rate of tax was 40 per cent than where it was 60 per cent. While cutting tax rates stimulates growth and brings in more revenue from the extra activity, there is usually some loss of revenue to begin with. In a world of controlled deficits and low growth from tight money policies, countries would have to find expenditure cuts to pay for the tax cuts. Experience has shown that this is very difficult. I have regularly argued for a lower rate of increase, but never for an actual reduction in total public spending. That is what would be needed to deliver a low-tax strategy in the world of Maastricht.

Socialists believe that high tax-and-spend would create more jobs. This would be possible under the Maastricht rules, but some of the spending to stimulate industry advocated by socialists would not be permissible. Grants and subsidies to companies are likely to be against the treaty, which rightly regards them as distortions in the market. While a socialist government could put taxes up and increase spending on health or welfare, it would have very limited scope for increasing spending on industrial aid under treaty rules.

The move to a single country is unlikely to gain the legitimacy and accountability needed to make it a success. In subsequent chapters we will examine the likely impact on jobs, inflation, growth and the other important economic matters. This chapter concludes that the lack of democratic control over monetary and economic policy would be a fatal flaw in the structure. People used to democracy would expect their politicians to interfere or change things unless the system was generating unprecedented economic success on a continuous basis.

Monetary union has to be seen in the context of a wish to create a superstate with wide-ranging governmental powers over a whole number of policies. A single state in Western Europe would flounder, as others have before, on the bewildering array of nationalities, races, religions and above all languages which characterize the rich European cultural inheritance. You could not make a single country speaking so many different languages; there could be no single country called Europe and no single government that would attract the loyalty and support of all the European peoples. But if we abolish the pound we make a decisive move towards a country called Europe, governed from Brussels and Frankfurt.

3

A Europe of the regions

The argument for monetary union has become part and parcel of the argument about a Europe of the regions. It has recently been vividly put by Umberto Bossi, the leader of the North Italian League. In September 1996 Mr Bossi led a demonstration across northern Italy and sailed into Venice to make his declaration of a northern Italian state. Proclaiming the need for a new country called Padania stretching from Turin to Venice along the Po Valley, Mr Bossi made it clear that he was a fan of the idea of a Europe of the regions. In the name of such a Europe he rejected the authority of Rome, demanded a self-governing Padania and welcomed further moves to European integration.

There is a similar gleam in the eye of the Catalan leadership in eastern Spain. They, too, would like looser links with Madrid or independence for Catalonia from the Spanish monarchy and Parliament. They, too, welcome the idea of a Europe of the regions, seeing in the European ideal a way of demolishing the powers of the Spanish state.

In the United Kingdom a minority of Scots takes the secessionist line. They wish to divorce Scotland from the rule of London and see in the concept of a Europe of the regions a device to help them in their cause against British power.

The unholy alliance between Brussels and these separatist movements is one that cannot last indefinitely. For the moment it is a marriage of convenience. The Brussels authorities and the regional movements have a common cause, to weaken or demolish central authority in the nation states of Western Europe. What will become apparent as they proceed is the fundamental incompatibility between those who believe that even a nation state is too large to govern them sensibly and those who wish to create a new superstate on the scale of the whole of Western Europe.

The claims of the Italian separatists in northern Italy are both economic and political. Northern Italy feels that southern Italy drags it down. At a time of economic failure, with high unemployment across Italy, the problem is particularly acute and pronounced in the south. As a result, in the unified state called Italy, the north has to pay higher taxes in order to send bigger transfer payments to the south to make up for the higher level of unemployment and social dislocation. This causes economic resentments.

Italy was only united in the nineteenth century; it looks back to a long and proud tradition of independent city states competing with one another. Go back further and Rome was the imperial power that conquered the other Italian states before going on to conquer much of Western Europe. With this background it is relatively easy for astute politicians in the north to whip up feelings against both Rome and the south as the unemployment queues lengthen.

The various kingdoms of Spain became one in the fifteenth century, at the reconquest of the country from the Moors. Catalonia, once a separate kingdom, still enjoys a different language and always saw itself as the most prosperous, bustling and commercial part of Spain. Barcelona is in many ways Spain's first city if measured by its commercial and trading importance. There has always been a strong argument between Barcelona and Madrid over how much government should come from the centre and how much should be left to Catalonia herself. The Spanish crisis has deepened with every step Spain has taken in recent years to try and bring her economy into line with the German one in preparation for monetary union. Starting from much lower levels of real income, productivity and technology, she has been through a rapid process of modernization. Now she is finding that the strict monetary requirements over debt, government deficits, inflation and interest rates have imposed terrible strains. Spain found it very difficult to keep the peseta within the Exchange Rate Mechanism, and in so doing precipitated a sharp decline in her economy. She is now burdened with 22 per cent unemployment, and with four out of ten of her young people without a job. This unrest about the state of the economy can easily be channelled into demands for regional separatism.

The Spanish kingdom was united through the reconquest from the Moors. Very disparate regions – Estremadura, Galicia, Granada, Castile, Catalonia, Mercia and Asturia – were welded together, united by one religion, Christianity, one currency , based on gold, and one monarchy. A federal structure was designed for parliamentary representation in the Cortes and strong senses of regional identity survived throughout. Separatist feeling was least pronounced when Spanish power and influence globally was at its peak but became more pronounced as the achievement of the Spanish kingdom waned.

Similar feelings are present within the United Kingdom. While England has been largely happy with the status of the United Kingdom as a single national entity, there have been endless arguments and debates about the role of Scotland, Ireland and to a lesser extent Wales within the unified United Kingdom. England herself has long been united under one crown with a single currency, a Christian Church and common governmental institutions. A common system of justice, parliamentary representation and local government has been in existence for many centuries.

Wales has been part of the combined kingdom for more than five hundred years. It was finally brought into union with England when a Welshman, Henry Tudor, became king of England. In recent times Welsh nationalists have never attracted more than one fifth of the popular vote and many of those who have nationalist inclinations would fall short of recommending the complete separation of Wales from England under its own independent government. When a lesser scheme of devolution was last proposed in the 1970s, suggesting an assembly in Wales to deal with Welsh issues under the sovereignty of the British parliament, even this was rejected decisively by the electorate.

The case of Scotland is said to be different. The union of the two crowns dates from the death of Elizabeth I in 1603, when James VI of Scotland succeeded to the English throne as James I. It was thus a Scottish king who made the historic decision to come to London and to govern from London. It was a Scottish king who saw the potential of the combined kingdom in European and international politics. In 1707 the Scottish Parliament agreed to a union of the parliaments and to most of the important powers of Scottish government passing to the sovereign United Kingdom parliament.

Despite the legacy of goodwill which the Scottish takeover of England created in Scotland and despite the obvious advantages of the combined kingdom to the Scottish people, particularly during the period of imperial success in the nineteenth and early twentieth centuries, there has been a strong movement against the current style of union in Scotland in recent years. There is still nothing like a majority who would like to see an entirely separate Scotland, severed from England and Wales. Scottish nationalists in general elections typically win three or four seats out of seventy-two Scottish seats in total, scarcely evidence of a landslide in favour of Scottish separation; even their manifestos usually fall short of demanding a complete separation of the two countries. When the issue of a devolved assembly was put to the Scottish people at the end of the 1970s a small majority of those voting favoured more devolved government in Scotland but under the rules, which required a minimum level of 40 per cent of the whole electorate in favour, the matter was not carried. The fact that many Scottish people refrained from voting at all indicated that it was not a burning concern to a majority of Scots at that point.

Ireland has been the most difficult area of the United Kingdom. A long and bitter history of conflict between Catholics and Protestants has continued to this day. In the earlier twentieth century it manifested itself in the form of a Catholic nationalist rising, leading

to the creation of a separate Republic of Ireland after the end of
the First World War. The conflict between the Protestant and
Catholic communities in Northern Ireland has continued. The
immediacy of the conflict over identity encourages stronger and
more extrovert British nationalism in the Protestant community
in Northern Ireland than is usually seen amongst the English on
the mainland. The threat to their continuing existence as part of
the United Kingdom makes them very staunch defenders of the
whole. The United Kingdom government has made it clear that as
long as a majority of the Ulster people wish to remain part of the
United Kingdom they will do so, but this does not meet with the
approval of radical nationalists who want to reunite Ireland.

The conclusion I come to is that the union of the United Kingdom,
although there are dissenters, remains the best way of organizing
the government of the different countries and regions of the union.
It is a democratic union. If any part of it developed a strong majority
view that they would be better off outside it, then a political way
would be found to bring this about peacefully. The deep roots of
the union in history account for its vitality and strength. England
is the best example of a stable, integrated, successful country in
the whole of Western Europe. The United Kingdom lays claim to
be one of a small group of relatively peaceful and stable countries.
France was convulsed by revolution only two hundred years ago.
Germany and Italy came together as countries only in the nineteenth century and have both had periods of fascist tyranny in the
twentieth. Spain is just recovering from fascism and a twentieth-
century civil war. Belgium is deeply divided between its Flemish-
and French-speaking parts. Luxembourg is a small enough country
for no further divisions to be possible and Holland has a unity
which comes from having thrown off Spanish and Hapsburg domination in the sixteenth century, a unity reinforced by the country's
Protestant religion.

It would be possible to get separatist and regional movements
going in many of these countries. In Spain the Catalan movement
is already well under way. In Spain and France the Basques have

for many years campaigned and even resorted to terrorism to try and create a separate country. In Belgium many would like to see two rather than one jurisdiction and in Germany the pull of the different parts is quite strong, with Brandenburg Prussia being very different in tone and feel from Bavaria or the western regions.

Those who favour the single currency often see these regional movements as their natural allies. In so doing they are playing with fire. We see an extreme example of what can happen in the former Yugoslavia. When the central communist control was removed, Yugoslavia began to split apart. It emerged that it was difficult to create a natural democracy that all the different religions and ethnic groups would regard as satisfactory. Yugoslavia split into Serbia, Croatia and Bosnia. In the recent Bosnian elections the electorate made clear that they felt Bosnia in turn should split into three, as each group felt it could not get justice or a satisfactory government by belonging to Bosnia as a whole.

Exponents of the single currency argue that these regional passions are there and cannot be suppressed. They see the regional passions as their natural allies, helping them to destroy the authority and legitimacy of national governments. They believe that people would naturally turn to the Frankfurt Central Bank and to the European single currency to provide the unifying economic policy and the common coinage. I think they will be bitterly disappointed if they do pursue this very dangerous route. The same forces that encourage Umberto Bossi in northern Italy to reject the authority of Rome would lead his successors to reject the authority of Brussels and Frankfurt. The main worry northern Italians have is that they are paying too high a price for their union with the south. If northern Italy were part of the European currency union, far from losing that burden they would gain new burdens, with obligations to other regions of Western Europe.

We must presume for these purposes that the southern Italy rump would apply for currency membership as well. Northern Italy would still therefore be in the same economic policy area, indeed in the same country as southern Italy but the country would now be called Europe rather than Italy. The problem would remain. Southern Italy would perform less well than northern Italy. Indeed, sharing an economic policy with Germany as well as with northern Italy might well make the problem worse, exacerbating the tight-money, high-unemployment policies that have characterized recent Italian and German experience. Far from lessening the burden of support, it might increase it. On top of that the more successful northern Italy would have to accept responsibilities towards eastern Germany, north-eastern France and other poorer parts of the currency union.

Creating a sense of nationhood is not the same as encouraging a crude nationalism that can be damaging to neighbours. A sense of nationhood means that people living in that country accept mutual responsibilities and obligations. A citizen of a nation or a subject of a monarchy accepts the rule of law of that country, participates in the common institutions to establish and uphold the law and accepts financial obligations to other members of that country's community. As a southern Englishman who believes in the union I fully accept British law. I would still accept British law if it were determined by a Labour government with a preponderance of Scottish, Welsh and northern English MPs. I accept the legitimacy of the system. I enjoy the freedom to oppose them and to seek to persuade the British people that it is better to elect a different type of government. When Conservatives lost in 1974 I campaigned for a future victory in a future election. I did not urge disobedience to the law or a change in the system.

Similarly, as a southern Englishman I accept that because my part of southern England is relatively more successful and prosperous than other parts of the United Kingdom, it is reasonable that we should pay more in tax so that there can be a decent level of benefits and support to people in parts of the country that are now less prosperous. I am quite happy at the thought that I will pay tax in order to help a blind person in Liverpool or an unemployed person in Glasgow. The sense of nationhood binds us together and we accept mutual obligations.

Such a sense of accountability and acceptance takes many centuries to nurture and bring to fruition. As we have seen in England, it has developed over a thousand years and in the United Kingdom over three hundred. I would not feel a similar sense of loyalty or sense of mutual obligation to people in Leipzig or Dresden or Calais or Sicily. If someone said to me that I should obey laws which had been primarily determined by elected members from continental countries I would disagree. I would want to change the system that perpetrated such an outrage. Similarly, if by virtue of a currency union I then had to accept obligations to pay higher taxes to look after unemployed young people in Sicily, or women on maternity leave in France, I would disagree. I do not have that sense of nationhood and shared purpose that I feel with fellow countrymen in the United Kingdom.

It is possible to have a strong sense of local or regional identity and a strong sense of nationhood. Many Welshmen are extremely proud to be Welsh. They are also proud of the United Kingdom and share a pride in the buildings and institutions of London as well as of Cardiff. Both work because both are based on a long history and evolution. It would be difficult to hold an equivalent loyalty to three levels, Wales, the United Kingdom and Europe. Those who favour a stronger sense of European identity in Wales are usually the same people who favour more or less radical change in the United Kingdom leading to a reduction of national power.

The single-currency scheme, if brought into being, could increase the sense of regional frustration rather than allaying it. What begins as an alliance between regionalism and federalism could soon deteriorate into a bitter conflict. Not only would the people of northern Italy find they had to pay bigger contributions to the poorer parts of the union, but they might also find that the economic policy being pursued by the Frankfurt Central Bank was even more hostile to their economic interests than the policies currently being pursued by the Italian government. True regional separatists should say 'No' to Brussels as well as to Rome.

The European Community is trying to counter this problem by

encouraging a sense of regional identity. In my own part of southern England they are trying to persuade us that we should have both a south-eastern regional identity and a Thames Valley identity. Neither of these makes much sense. Their south-eastern region excludes London yet London lies at the heart of the south-eastern region. If you ask people to define the Thames Valley even those of us who live in it would have great difficulty in defining its boundaries or borders. The Thames Valley is a geographical, not a political, fact of life. We understand Berkshire, Oxfordshire, Hampshire. These are long-standing counties that have been reflected in local government, the dispensation of justice, in cricket teams and road signs.

A propaganda booklet printed for the European Commission delves into history to establish European connections. We are told, 'Roman and Norman links are evident across the sub-region [the south-east of England] to show that the ties with Europe stretch far back into history.' There is no explanation that these 'links' were the result of invasion and military settlement – hardly a good way to encourage a sense of European togetherness.

The EC thinks it can make regions out of a few leaflet drops, brochures and grant programmes. The same brochure seems almost to regret that the south-east is by and large a prosperous area, but cheers up when it finds pockets of unemployment and deprivation which can be touched by Euro-grants. The deeper motive oozes from every sentence: the EC wants to undermine the nation in order to build a bigger one.

PART 2
THE ECONOMICS

4

The Exchange Rate Mechanism

According to the Maastricht Treaty, joining the Exchange Rate Mechanism and keeping a stable rate within it for two years is an essential precondition for any country wishing to join the single currency. The scheme originally designed at Maastricht goes back to earlier visions of how a single currency should be brought about. It was always assumed that it would take place by pegging currencies one to another in an exchange-rate grid or snake, with the permitted variations reducing over time until it was a relatively straightforward step to substitute for all the differently named member-state currencies the single common currency or the ecu, a basket of them.

In 1989 an active debate was conducted in the United Kingdom as to whether Britain should join the Exchange Rate Mechanism or not. We had one brief experience in the earlier version of the ERM, the snake, under Sir Edward Heath as Prime Minister in the early 1970s. Our membership was short-lived. The foreign-exchange pressures built up very quickly on sterling and it was soon thrown out of the system.

By 1989 the Confederation of British Industry, the Labour Party, leading members of the Conservative Cabinet, many commentators, economists and journalists, all strongly supported going into the Exchange Rate Mechanism. They argued that we should be able to keep our currency stable against the Deutschmark, and that by doing so we would mirror Germany's performance in creating a low-inflation economy. Many felt that it would create greater stability. They pointed to the erratic inflation rates experienced in the United Kingdom in the postwar period compared with the lower and more stable inflation rate of Germany and concluded that Britain would be better advised to steer her monetary policy by the Deutschmark than by her own domestic decisions.

Just before I joined the government in 1989 I wrote a pamphlet on Europe which set out the case against joining the Exchange Rate Mechanism. I was worried even at that stage that our monetary policy was being debauched by shadowing the Deutschmark. Although we had not formally entered the ERM the Treasury had decided that keeping the pound relatively stable against the Deutschmark was a better course of counter-inflationary action than proceeding with the Medium Term Financial Strategy and monetary targeting, which had been the method successfully used in the early to mid 1980s.

I discussed the academic support for membership of the ERM and pointed out that even the academic commentators in favour of it conceded that ERM stability for continental currencies had been made easier by capital and exchange controls limiting the free movement of monies. The abolition of these controls as part of the 1992 single-market programme made ERM convergence more difficult. They also argued that because sterling was such a widely traded international currency it would be more difficult to keep it within the narrow bands than smaller, less-well-traded currencies like the florin or the Belgian franc.

I argued that the ERM was likely to destabilize rather than stabilize the British economy. I stated:

The idea of the EMS is theoretically flawed. The history of the pound against the Deutschmark over the last year [1988] illustrates why this is so. Despite government efforts to get the pound to shadow the Deutschmark and to hold it around the level of 3 Deutschmarks to the pound, there have been periods of intense pressure leading to substantial fluctuations around that level.

The main method for trying to keep the currencies in line is the sale or purchase of quantities of given currency by the European central banks acting in concert or individually. If people find the pound particularly attractive compared with the Deutschmark, all the central banks sell pounds and buy Deutschmarks in an effort to counter the substantial commercial forces ranged on the other side. This action is intrinsically destabilizing. If the Bank of England sells a large amount of sterling in order to buy Deutschmarks it then has a monetary problem. If it simply creates the pounds it has sold it adds directly to the money supply. Foreign banks and other buyers then have more pounds at their disposal. If they go into the banking system these become high-powered money, enabling a bank to lend this money several times over, expanding the amount of sterling credit in circulation. This produces upward pressure on the British price level, causing inflationary worries and forcing a further rise in interest rates. Once there has been a further increase in interest rates, sterling then looks even more attractive from the point of view of the overseas purchaser, leading to a further demand for pounds, requiring more pounds to be manufactured and sold by the Bank of England!

The origins of the great inflation in Britain in the early 1990s lie in the attempts to shadow the Deutschmark in the later 1980s. Because at that point sterling was an attractive currency and wanted to go up against the Deutschmark, efforts to keep it down ballooned the money supply in the United Kingdom in the way I described. A credit explosion occurred in the late 1980s with billions of pounds of extra money being made available by the banks to lenders as a direct result of the high-powered money created through the perverse consequences of the monetary policy followed in the name of stabilizing the exchange rate. I went on to explain it in a little more detail:

The bank does have some means of trying to offset this monetary problem. It puts itself into the ridiculous position of selling large quantities of gilt-edged securities to the private sector in order to counteract the monetary expansion caused by the intervention. In the year to March 1988 the government, which collected £3,600m more in taxes than it spent on public goods and services, had none the less to borrow an additional £7,000m through the gilt-edged market in order to counter-balance the short-term monetary consequences of trying to shadow the Deutschmark. This has burdened British tax payers for twenty to twenty-five years with an additional £700m a year of interest charges. Against this the Bank of England has acquired claims on Germany and Japan that offer very low rates of interest . . . if the British authorities had not been trying to shadow the Deutschmark, monetary interest rates and even exchange-rate policy might have been more stable. Let us assume in the quarter to March 1988 the government had bought no Deutschmarks or yen. Instead of needing to borrow to counteract the monetary effects of issuing more pounds, the government could have repaid debt, further strengthening its strong financial position and cutting the interest burden in subsequent years. As a result of issuing less new debt and having better monetary control, interest rates would have remained at a lower level. In consequence, the pound would have been slightly less attractive to overseas buyers and might, therefore, have risen less fast and less far then it did under the interventionist scheme.

Unfortunately the damage was done. The credit explosion occurred, in no small measure because Britain was selling pounds and creating pounds in order to try and keep the value of the pound down. This in turn triggered an inflation which then needed drastic monetary action to correct it. Broad money was growing by 15–16 per cent a year. While the financial statement in the *Budget Report* proudly concluded, 'Sterling has shown considerable stability against the Deutschmark over the past year,' it had to skate over the fact that money and credit had grown at close to 16 per cent in twelve months (M4). Despite this massive increase in credit the Treasury concluded that inflation would remain under good control. They must have been concentrating on the stability of the exchange rate rather than looking at what really mattered, the massive expansion of credit they had unleashed as a result of their intervention across the exchanges and their relaxed attitude towards the growth of credit in the banking system.

A year later in March 1989 the *Financial Statement and Budget Report* had to report a further increase in money and credit growth to 17 per cent (M4). Inflation had soared to 6 per cent by the fourth quarter of 1988 but the Treasury, looking at the exchange rate and narrow money, was again saying that inflation would fall decisively by the middle of 1990. The Treasury continued its redefinition of its policy. It stated, 'The exchange rate is a key influence on, and a key indicator of, monetary conditions. It has to be considered together with all the evidence of domestic indicators in making monetary-policy decisions. Monetary policy has the overriding task of defeating inflation: the government is accordingly not prepared to accommodate increases and domestic costs by exchange-rate depreciation. Sterling has risen slightly against the Deutschmark over the past year. The dollar has also risen against the Deutschmark, though it has shown little change against the yen.' Gradually, almost imperceptibly, the Treasury moved away from the middle 1980s position of controlling the growth of credit and broad money in the economy to targeting the exchange rate as their main means of guiding policy. As a result they completely misjudged the likely move in inflation and undermined the stability the British economy had experienced in the period 1981–6. Far from declining as they hoped, inflation soared to 10 per cent by the fourth quarter of 1990.

The Treasury went on to say in its March 1989 statement that 'Exchange rates are also important in international economic relations. The improved cooperation between the G7 countries, who share a common counter-inflation objective, has been clearly beneficial to the international community.' It was at this juncture in British policy that policy-makers were not only interested in international cooperation at the European level through shadowing the ERM but also in cooperation with the Japanese and American authorities in a kind of super ERM including the yen and the dollar as well as the principal European currencies. They mesmerized each other into believing that greater currency stability would prevent inflation. Greater currency stability between countries all experiencing rising inflation does not curb inflation at all and can be very misleading.

Any student of the ERM period in British economics and politics must understand that there was an important shift of policy in the later 1980s before we entered the ERM properly. As the Treasury *Guidance Notes* and their action makes clear, Britain was trying to keep the pound at around 3 Deutschmarks throughout the later 1980s. As a result, because the pound wished to go up, far too many pounds were printed and created and sold across the exchanges. Far too many of these found their way back through the British banking system and helped create a big credit explosion. This credit explosion at the end of the 1980s was not checked by proper monetary action. The Treasury took its eye off the ball. It saw a strong exchange rate, which it found very reassuring. It argued that if sterling was strong there could be no recurrence of inflation. The damage was done and inflation soared from the acceptable levels of the mid 1980s to double figures by the early 1990s. Had the original Medium Term Financial Strategy with a broad money target been continued in the later 1980s, none of this would have happened.

It was on 8 October 1990 that the United Kingdom decided to join the ERM. Having tried to keep the pound down to around 2.95 Deutschmarks, its chosen central rate in the ERM in the later 1980s, this was the chosen rate for entering the ERM in October 1990. It was some way off the peak. Sterling had reached almost 3.3 Deutschmarks during the period of intense pressure in the late 1980s. The government patiently waited for it to come back to what they thought was a sensible sustainable rate. It was an average rate that the pound had sustained over quite a long time period, from the middle of 1986 onwards. Indeed it was the rate that they had clearly been trying to create and sustain during those years of proxy membership of the ERM.

The Treasury explained the impact of the ERM in its 1991/2 *Financial Statement and Budget Report.* 'Interest rates remain the essential instrument of monetary policy, but now the overriding factor in setting them is the need to meet the United Kingdom's ERM obligations.' This was only a matter of degree, as monetary policy in the two or three years prior to entry had clearly been primarily determined by the wish to keep sterling in line with the

Deutschmark. Now it was an open public commitment, however, the pressure on the policy-makers to make it work intensified. Any failure would entail a major loss of face.

The Treasury went on to explain, 'Any loss of discretion to respond to domestic monetary conditions is likely to be more than compensated for by the improved market confidence and reduced inflationary expectations that the ERM commitment is bringing about.' Britain decided to join the wider bands of the ERM. As then constituted the mechanism allowed members of the wider bands to deviate by plus or minus 6 per cent around their central rate. Those currencies in the narrow bands were only permitted a 2¼ percentage-point deviation either side of their central rate. By the time sterling entered the ERM formally the pressures were more likely to be downwards than upwards. As a result of the proxy ERM period of monetary policy Britain had experienced soaring inflation and had then had to raise interest rates dramatically to try and curb the credit boom. Just prior to entering the ERM interest rates were at 15 per cent. As part of the deal Margaret Thatcher insisted on a one percentage-point drop in short-term interest rates in return for joining the ERM. Britain therefore entered and posted short-term interest rates at 14 per cent.

The case of those who favoured entry into the ERM was positive, glowing and encouraging; they said that entering would enable us to enjoy a 'golden scenario'. The golden scenario would mean that interest rates could come down, economic growth could be resumed and inflation would fall to low levels, where it would remain. They had every confidence that the British economy could be brought into line with the German economy and that the German economy would remain an anchor economy combining good growth with low inflation.

Some of us never saw how this was going to work. The German and British economies were at different stages of the cycle. The British economy was going into recession while the German economy was still expanding. Added to this were the complications associated with German reunification. At exactly the point where

Britain decided to link her fortunes irrevocably and publicly to the Deutschmark the German authorities decided to debauch the Deutschmark by going in for a precipitous and generous currency union with East Germany. It did not matter that the German central bank argued against this. It did not matter that informed commentators around the world said that a currency union of the two Germanies on generous terms to the East Germans would be inflationary, effectively printing new Deutschmarks not supported by the economic endeavour of the Eastern Länder.

None the less the exponents of the golden scenario held to their ground. With considerable difficulty the government managed to edge interest rates down during our period in the ERM, although they remained well above the levels that British industry and commerce could sustain as the recession intensified. In March 1992 the Treasury explained that membership of the ERM was necessary to meet the convergence criteria of the Maastricht Treaty. 'ERM membership will remain the central discipline underpinning United Kingdom macro-economic policy in a medium term.' The Treasury was confident that with a little more pain and a little more pressure, and some further continuation of high interest rates, the period of adjustment would be over. The Treasury briefed ministers to tell people that the recession would be relatively shallow and short-lived, and that recovery would follow quite rapidly after the General Election in the spring of 1992. The public was extremely sceptical about this. By now a long period of high interest rates, needed to correct the credit explosion of the late 1980s, was bankrupting businesses, driving house prices down and doing all sorts of economic damage. None the less the Treasury looked to the future and stated, 'Sterling will move to narrow bounds within the ERM in due course, maintaining its central rate at 2.95 Deutschmarks.'

With the General Election out of the way and the Conservative government duly re-elected, the recession intensified. Instead of the predictions of recovery coming true, the British economy struggled to deal with the very high interest rates needed to main-

tain sterling's position in the ERM. By the autumn of 1992 speculators began to decide that the pain inflicted on the British economy
was too great and that sterling would have to leave the ERM. The
government was reluctant to accept defeat. It threw everything
into the battle. Millions of pounds of foreign-exchange reserves
were sold across the exchanges in order to buy up pounds in the
hope that this would bolster the value of sterling. It was decided
that interest rates had to be increased. On the final day in the
ERM interest rates were hoisted to 12 per cent and a beleaguered
Chancellor of the Exchequer said that they would return to 15 per
cent the following morning. It was a sign that he was prepared to
try anything, to demonstrate the government's commitment to
the ERM, to appease the markets, to persuade them that the pound
would be defended.

Unfortunately it was all to no avail. The market forces were
simply too great. Spending foreign-exchange reserves on buying
up pounds did the opposite of what was needed. Every £100m
bought up removed credit from the system. At a time when
businesses were desperate for more bank lending to keep them
going through very difficult trading conditions, banks instead
had to call in their loans and cut their credit in response to the
purchase and destruction of pounds through foreign-exchange
intervention. The country had to borrow billions of pounds of convertible foreign currencies in order to buy up sterling. As a
result the taxpayer was lumbered with further debts. Despite
billions of pounds of foreign-exchange intervention, despite the
two increases in interest rates, despite the strong government
commitment to the ERM, on 16 September 1992 they decided to
give in and accept that market forces were too strong for them.
The damage done was considerable. The years 1991 and 1992
saw falls in national income and output. Unemployment soared to
three million. Thousands of businesses went bankrupt. There was
endless bad news about redundancies, closed companies and struggling enterprises.

The British economy needed much lower interest rates, some

credit growth, a substantial easing of the pain. This came quite rapidly once we had removed ourselves from the ERM. By March 1993 the Treasury could report short-term interest rates down to 6 per cent, the lowest rates in the European Community. The long-term interest rates had fallen one point from the February 1992 level. Monetary policy had changed again, for the better.

The Treasury stated, 'Last autumn, following the suspension of sterling's membership of the ERM, the government put in place a new policy framework for its counter-inflation strategy.' While it is a little ominous that the Treasury only talks about the suspension of sterling's membership, probing questions in the House of Commons persuaded the Prime Minister to confirm that the government had no intention of re-entering the mechanism in the lifetime of the 1992–7 Parliament. As a result, of course, the government needed a new economic policy framework. The Treasury went on to state, 'While the pound remains outside the ERM, decisions about interest rates are based on a continuing assessment of monetary conditions, measured principally by the growth of narrow and broad money, and movements in the exchange rate and asset prices.' This was a very sensible new policy. The idea that broad money, a way of looking at credit expansion generally, did matter and should have an impact on monetary policy brought the system back to some common sense. What the Treasury had known in the middle 1980s, and had deliberately forgotten in the later 1980s and early 1990s in its pursuit of the Deutschmark, was restored to an important place in policy-making. As a result it was possible to set interest rates that made sense for British industry and commerce.

The plunging interest rates and the modest increase in credit eased the pressures on the business community dramatically. Unemployment started to fall month by month. Slowly business confidence started to rebuild and the economy began to grow again. The Treasury feared that inflation would pick up because of the devaluation, but the subsequent couple of years demonstrated that this was totally ungrounded. Inflation was not going to pick up then, because credit had been very strongly controlled during our period in the ERM and could continue to be controlled while the government followed a sensible monetary policy.

By November 1994 the Treasury could state, 'Sterling has remained stable against a basket of currencies this year, although it has appreciated against the dollar and depreciated against the main European currencies and the yen.' Of course, immediately on leaving the ERM there was a sharp downward movement in sterling against the Deutschmark and Deutschmark-related currencies. Several other European currencies also succumbed to the same pressures at the same time. The escudo, the lira, the peseta, the Finnish markka and the Swedish krona all devalued. It was not a sterling crisis. It was more a Deutschmark crisis, with the Deutschmark wishing to go up and the other currencies taking the strain. The German central bank put everything into the defence of the franc but was not so willing to defend the other currencies of the system.

On leaving the ERM, Britain was able to follow a policy geared to the interests of the domestic and exporting economy. One of the big problems had been the discovery that the Deutschmark might drag the pound to a value against the dollar which did not suit Britain's trade. Britain has a large trade in dollar-denominated products. For example, aerospace products, computer products and other high-tech industrial goods are commonly priced in dollars. As a leading exporter in these industries and a leading location for American companies based in Europe, Britain needed a pound competitive against the dollar in order to carry on trading successfully in these products. During the period of Deutschmark strength in 1991–2 the pound was dragged to unrealistic levels against the dollar, doing considerable damage to the exports and the industrial capability of these important industries.

It also hit our tourism. American tourists often prefer to come to London and the United Kingdom rather than continental centres when visiting Europe; the common language, history and culture is one of the principal attractions. By the middle of 1992, however, there was a notable shortage of American tourists in London, as the pound had been dragged up too high against the dollar, and London had become too expensive.

We also learnt in our ERM period that the forces of speculators are considerably stronger than the money and power available even to central banks and governments working in concert: the volumes of money traded across the exchanges every day vastly exceed the reserves of even the richest countries. If the market-places decide that a currency is too high or too low there is little that the concerted intervention of central banks can do about it. Even a government prepared to hike interest rates to totally unacceptable levels in the middle of the recession, even a government prepared to borrow billions of pounds to shore up its currency position, was unable to defend its currency against speculative pressures.

Thirdly, we should have learnt that the ERM was destabilizing rather than stabilizing. Given the inflationary pressures created by shadowing the Deutschmark in the late 1980s, interest rates undoubtedly had to be raised and a period of credit tightening was necessary. The problem was that the credit tightening and period of high interest rates was exaggerated by the need to maintain sterling's value against the Deutschmark. Had we been following a domestic policy, we would have lowered interest rates earlier. This would not have done damage to the inflationary position. The subsequent performance of inflation from 1993 to 1996 was exemplary. Only four years after leaving the ERM we could proudly report the lowest rate of inflation since the 1950s. This had come about through cautious and tight monetary policies, pursued even after we had left the ERM, in parallel with a most welcome and necessary reduction in interest rates to provide some easing of the restrictions on the British economy.

Unfortunately, joining the ERM does not offer a surefire way of guaranteeing low inflation or stable policy. As we have seen, it was following the Deutschmark in the 1980s which caused the inflation, which membership of the ERM then corrected through the stringency it required. It would have been possible and desirable to have followed a more stable policy without reference to the Deutschmark rate throughout the 1980s and 1990s.

What relevance does the ERM experience have to those considering joining a single currency? It should be seen as central evidence in the case. The single-currency proponents are effectively recycling the old golden scenario that ERM exponents produced in the later 1980s. What is surprising is that they are prepared to try again when the experience with the ERM was so bitter. The exponents of the single currency say that it will remove currency fluctuations, lower inflationary expectations and build business confidence. They believe that because the currency area is bigger that somehow makes it better and more stable.

On the contrary, joining a single currency is like rejoining the ERM but throwing away the key to the locked door. Imagine what would have happened in September 1992 if we had not been able to get out of the ERM: George Soros and other international currency traders sold pounds until the rate had to be changed; interest rates would have gone up further to defend the pound; the recessionary forces in the economy would have been intensified; far from unemployment coming down and business confidence growing, the reverse would have happened. The exponents of the single currency say the absence of George Soros and the speculative hordes working away against sterling, had we joined the single currency, would mean that belonging to the single currency would be completely different. They miss the fundamental point. If you give away the opportunity to allow the exchange rate to take the strain, the strain of adjustment will inevitably fall on the real economy. Instead of the sterling rate changing, factories close, people lose their jobs and the adjustment process is that much more painful.

Nor is it possible to divorce belonging to the ERM from the single currency. It is a condition of joining the single currency that a country should have led a stable life in the ERM for two years prior to entry. The Community has always stuck to its view that the best way to a single currency is to demonstrate ever-growing convergence of the currencies that wish to join.

The Dublin summit of 1996 reconfirmed this by establishing the second ERM. This, we are told, is a different mechanism from the one it replaces. Rather than being based on cross-rates from one currency to the others it is based on a hub-and-spoke principle, tied to a central rate to the euro. This is playing with words. If each currency has a fixed exchange rate to the central currency in the system then you can also work out the cross-rates between all the currencies in the system. Similarly, in the old ERM had you nominated a currency, the ecu, as the anchor of the system it would have been possible to work out the rate to that. The essential characteristics of the two mechanisms are the same. They are based upon the proposition that the participating currencies must stay within narrow bands of each other. They are based on the proposition that central banks must make their prime aim of policy the establishment of stable currencies against the other member currencies. They assume that the combined powers of the central banks and governments will outstrip the combined powers of the speculators and they assume that the economies and currencies are sufficiently converged to be able to live happily together. The only problem is that there is no evidence whatsoever that the currencies and economies have sufficiently converged to live harmoniously together in this way.

Between 1983 and 1987 gross national income rose by 14 per cent. Price inflation was at or below 5 per cent and sterling stayed on average at around $1.50 to the pound. It is true there had been currency fluctuations, but the general performance of the economy was stable. There was good average growth year on year, unemployment was coming down and inflation was under reasonable control. Between 1987 and 1993 we had a period of intense turbulence. Growth shot up, inflation shot up and the economy was then plunged into a deep recession. Inflation shot down, unemployment rose dramatically and a lot of damage was done to British business. The first period is the period of the Medium

Term Financial Strategy, driven by control of broad and narrow money and a pragmatic approach to running the economy. The second period is the period of ideological commitment to the sterling/Deutschmark rate. The results of the experiment are very clear for all to see. The ERM was destabilizing, the pragmatic Medium Term Financial Strategy was friendly to growth and development of the economy. Since 1992 we have returned to most of the virtues of a pragmatic Medium Term Financial Strategy. As a result we have seen another era of good growth, low inflation and falling unemployment.

Advocates of the single currency say that the absence of speculative pressures makes all the difference. They are right in one respect. If we abolish the pound then the British government could not be driven into extreme measures to defend the pound's value. However, if we were in a single currency, in many other respects it would be the same as being in the ERM without the right to get out. Monetary policy would be set in the general interests of the union as a whole. If the union is not a reasonably homogenous area with common economic activity, then the interest rate set overall might be too lax or too severe for the British part of the union. Britain would feel what some in Scotland felt in 1988/9, when the Scottish economy was doing less well than the English economy, and yet Scotland had to cope with the higher interest rates needed for the United Kingdom as a whole. This could often be the position Britain would face in a currency union with our continental partners.

Advocates of currency union say that this means Britain wishes to maintain devaluation as an option. That is not my position at all. I want us to keep open the option of making the appropriate adjustment, whether it be upwards or downwards, through the currency rather than through some more direct and painful means. Given the pattern of Britain's trade it is not only the Deutschmark rate that matters to us. Getting the wrong value of our currency against the dollar can be even more damaging. In the late 1980s I did not wish us to pursue the devaluation option: I wished us to pursue the revaluation option. Had we in the late 1980s allowed sterling to rise more rapidly than we did, we could have avoided some of the excesses and problems we experienced. Conversely, when the Deutschmark was too strong in 1992, of course it would have been better to have allowed the pound to devalue against the Deutschmark but to keep a sensible value against the dollar.

During our period in the ERM businesses were told they must immediately cut their wage increases, raise their productivity and bring their performance into line with Germany. The transition was too sharp. British conditions are not the same as German. In some respects they are better and in some respects less favourable. The exchange rate allows adjustments to take place at a more realistic rate.

Many who favour European integration look back on the ERM experience and say that what was wrong was the initial rate at which we entered. At least they concede – as does everyone in the debate – that the British government tried everything in its power in August and September 1992 to try and save the pound. No one suggests we should have squandered or borrowed even more billions in an effort to sustain an unsustainable sterling.

The argument that 2.95 Deutschmarks to the pound was the wrong rate is a very curious one. It was not an argument made by the advocates of ERM entry at the time. When we entered, people commented on how wise the government had been in waiting for sterling to come back some 10 per cent from its high against the Deutschmark over the previous year before fixing the rate. Commentators felt that it was a sensible rate to go in at, based on the average rate that we had experienced for many months before making the decision to go public. As we have seen it was related to the rate the Treasury had been using for many months in their efforts to shadow the German currency.

It is true that the advocates of entry knew that in order to make it work there had to be a change in price and wage behaviour by British businesses. They made that very clear, and many businesses tried to respond. What were the other options available to the

British government? Given that they wanted to enter the ERM at that time, there were not many. They could have chosen a rate 5 or 10 pfennigs lower than the one they chose. Given that the pound fell 15 per cent against the Deutschmark in September 1992 on exit from the ERM, 5 or 10 pfennigs either way would probably have not made very much difference to the eventual outcome. Had the government tried to devalue the pound on entry, one of two things would have happened. Either people would have taken the devaluation as a strong signal that the British government was not serious about the discipline of the ERM and as a confession by the British government that they felt Britain was really too weak to sustain its obligations, or the markets would not have believed the devaluation and would have immediately placed sterling under upward pressure, trying to break it out of the bands in an upwards direction. Neither of these proposals recommended itself to the government at the time.

The only other possibility would have been for the government to have delayed entry in the hope that sterling would fall further against the Deutschmark, until one day it found a level which they thought would be sustainable. But there is no right rate for sterling against the Deutschmark which you can fix and hold in perpetuity. The long history of sterling against the Deutschmark, the dollar, the yen and any other major world currency is one of fluctuations and trend movements. In the postwar period sterling has been in a downwards trend against the Deutschmark; in the interwar period sterling was in a pronounced upward trend against the then German currency.

There is a correct rate today for sterling against the Deutschmark and there will be another correct rate in three months' time but it will be a remarkable coincidence if these two rates are the same. The purpose of the exchange rate is to allow people to exchange German currency freely for British currency or vice versa. It is a market like any other and the price adjusts according to the balance of buyers and sellers. They take into account their views on how well or badly the British and German economies are performing and whether or not the British and German monetary authorities are equally serious about keeping the value of their money and curbing inflation. The best way for the British authorities to keep the value of the pound high against the Deutschmark, if that is their main aim, is to pursue tight control of credit and inflation at home so that people gain confidence in the currency. You do not have to belong to an exchange-rate mechanism to do this.

Those who would like us to join the single currency must be contemplating our re-entry into the ERM in order to qualify. Should we go back in at today's rate of 2.70 Deutschmarks, 25 pfennigs lower than the rate in the 1990–92 period? We might take comfort from the fact that it is sensibly lower than the rate which proved unsustainable in September 1992. Or, because more recent trading experience of the pound has seen it at between 2.20 and 2.40 Deutschmarks, should we devalue to that level to re-enter? Or perhaps we should wait until the pound has retraced some of its steps to nearer 2.30 or 2.40 Deutschmarks? To pose a question in this way should show anyone how foolish is the idea that there is a correct rate. If we went in at today's rate and the upward pressures on sterling continue we might repeat the experiences of the late 1980s. We would be printing pounds and selling them across the exchanges to try and keep the pound down, thereby fuelling the credit explosion which is already gathering momentum anyway through domestic policy. Alternatively, the German economy might start to improve and Chancellor Kohl might decide to give up his policy of a weaker Deutschmark. If that happened, then we might find that having entered at 2.70 Deutschmarks to the pound it proved difficult to sustain the other way and we would repeat the problems of 1991 and 1992.

If you follow a policy based on taking a clear view of how much credit there should be in your own economy and what inflation rate you wish to allow you have a chance of success. If you gear your policy to shadowing somebody else's currency then your own domestic economy is subject to the vagaries and random events that other countries' policies can create. It was not Britain's choice that Chancellor Kohl decided to debauch the Deutschmark in the early 1990s by the currency union of the two Germanies, but as Germany sucked in more and more credit and more and more money to fuel the rebuilding of Eastern Germany, so more and more pressure was placed on the pound. Today, the main German political requirement is the need to ease pressure on France and Germany herself in the interests of moving quickly towards currency union. As a result Chancellor Kohl has influenced or overridden the German central bank in the interests of a looser German monetary policy and a lower Deutschmark. If Britain rejoined the ERM she would find her own policy came under the influence of that policy. While it may well be right for Germany to loosen her monetary policy, create more credit and lower interest rates, with a view to getting the German economy to grow again, it would be quite wrong for Britain, with a much more advanced economic recovery and a credit boom already under way. Now is the time to follow a firmer policy than Germany's, not to follow a policy as lax as Germany's.

There is no single right rate for the pound against the Deutschmark. Re-entering the ERM would destabilize the British economy again, for the mechanism is intrinsically destabilizing: instead of controlling the economy in the interests of domestic business and the domestic price level you have to cope with random events from overseas. The British economy suffers enough shocks of its own without having to mimic those imposed on the German economy by German politicians. It is most important that British governments continue to confirm that Britain will not join the ERM. If we do not rejoin it we can pursue a more sensible domestic policy geared to our own growth and prosperity. If we do not rejoin the ERM we cannot possibly qualify for the single currency. The single currency is like rejoining the ERM, locking yourself in and throwing away the key.

5

How states would lose control of their budgets

Monetary union entails passing substantial control over economic policy to European institutions. Proponents of the single currency imply that it is a technical matter: yet it is fundamental, and goes to the heart of what government can do.

The treaty clearly states that, 'Member states shall avoid excessive government deficits' in Article 104c. The treaty is right to highlight this crucial issue. If different member states persevered with differing levels of deficits under a common currency scheme, a high-borrowing state would take advantage of the lower-borrowing ones.

The rate of interest at which a government borrows is related to the amount it needs to borrow and to the likely future value of the currency. In a single-currency area, currency variability has been removed, and all borrow at a similar interest rate. At the moment, with fourteen different national currencies, each state borrows at a different interest rate based on the market's view of its creditworthiness, the amount it wants to borrow and the likely strength of its currency. In the single-currency scheme, if member states could carry on borrowing as much as they liked, a high-borrowing country would help drive up the rate of interest for all the countries, as the markets would look at the creditworthiness and quantity of borrowing of the governments as a whole, being unable to set different interest rates for different currencies. They might differentiate between the creditworthiness of the different governments, but the difference would be insignificant in normal circumstances.

Naturally the union feels there must be some limit on the profligate to protect the prudent, and to keep union interest rates down to sensible levels. The treaty sets out an elaborate procedure to do just this. It states:

The Commission shall monitor the development of the budgetary situation and of the stock of government debt in the member states with a view to identifying gross errors. In particular it shall examine compliance with budgetary discipline on the basis of the following two criteria:

(a) whether the ratio of the planned or actual government deficit to gross domestic product exceeds a reference value, unless

either the ratio has declined substantially and continuously and reached a level that comes close to the reference value;

or, alternatively, the excess over the reference value is only exceptional and temporary and the ratio remains close to the reference value;

(b) whether the ratio of government debt to gross domestic product exceeds a reference value, unless the ratio is sufficiently diminishing and approaching the reference value at a satisfactory pace.

These requirements are better defined in the Protocol on excessive deficits attached to the treaty, which specifies that the annual government deficit should not be more than 3 per cent of gross domestic product, and that the stock of government debt should not exceed 60 per cent of GDP.

Although there are some weasel words and some elements of judgement involved in deciding on whether a country qualifies or not, the scope is somewhat limited by the drafting. If a country has been running a deficit of 5 per cent of its national output for some time it is difficult to see how it could qualify. If a country has debt equivalent to 80 per cent or more of its GDP, surely it could not be inside. A country which had got its stock of debt down to 65 per cent and still falling might be all right, as might a country whose deficit was running at 3.5 per cent that year but would be below 3 per cent in later years.

At the moment these criteria exclude most European countries from qualifying. There seems no prospect of Italy, Greece or Belgium, for example, lowering their debt/GDP ratios sufficiently, given that they are all above 100 per cent, or Sweden at 80 per cent. Portugal and Spain seem unlikely to reduce their budget deficits to below 3 per cent in time.

Even France and Germany are struggling to reduce their budget deficits to 3 per cent. We should expect flexible interpretation of the clauses concerning progress towards the targets to be coupled with some creative accounting to come to their aid. Already countries are examining ways of taking obligations off the balance sheet, or receiving money in return for accepting longer-term obligations, to lower the deficit in the qualifying years. For example, the French have raised money by accepting obligations to pay Telecom pensions in future years. The first year looks better, but later years will look worse as a result. Some think parts of the Belgian debt may be redefined as non-state debt.

If a member state does have an excessive deficit or is likely to run one, the Commission under the treaty has to take action. The Commission prepares a report which it presents to the monetary committee established under the treaty. The committee gives an opinion on the Commission finding, which is then put to the Council of Ministers. The Council ultimately decides if the Commission is correct, voting by qualified majority on whether there is or is not an excessive deficit. If there is, the Council makes proposals to the member state to correct the deficit.

If the member state then fails to sort things out, the Council can publish its findings and recommendations, in the hope that public pressure will force the necessary adjustments. If the member state still fails to comply, the Council can instruct it to do so, and demand reports on how it is getting on. In the last resort, the Council can invite the European Investment Bank to reconsider its lending policy towards the member state concerned; it can require a non-interest-bearing deposit to be lodged, or it can impose fines.

These are draconian powers. If properly enforced, it means that member states would be unable to borrow more than 3 per cent of their GDP in any year, and would be unable to make any new borrowings at all if they have reached an outstanding debt equal to 60 per cent of their GDP. All this would be enforced by escalating from public shame to deposits and fines sufficiently large to force the member state to back down.

Many will say that a member state should not want to borrow more, and that living within these generous limits is neither unreasonable nor difficult. Yet twelve of the fifteen member states already have a stock of borrowing above the limits of the treaty and would be unable to borrow at all. Although I favour borrowing less, and keeping debt levels down, I think it too draconian to say to a country like Austria or Germany that you cannot borrow a single euro more because your stock of debt is already too high.

Some argue that these sections of the treaty will not be enforced like that, in which case it is curious that these matters were thought to be important enough to be written into the treaty in 1992, and that fans of the scheme can casually say that embarrassing treaty provisions can be overturned. If Europe is to avoid a lawyers' feast and a litigants' nightmare, either the rules of the treaty must be enforced, or the treaty must be amended properly to accommodate a different view.

For most countries the inability to borrow would come as a great shock. In the postwar world governments are accustomed to borrowing, sometimes justifying it by saying they are adding to the nation's capital assets. In recognition of this the Commission report is allowed to take investment expenditure into account. In all probability it would mean some relaxation of the intent of the treaty. The system would then become arbitrary. The real power to decide budgets would rest with the Commission, who would have to report and recommend to the Council. The Council itself proceeds by qualified majority voting to decide if there is an excessive deficit and, by two-thirds majority excluding the affected member state, to impose penalties.

For any individual country the flexibility might come to be an intrusion rather than welcome common sense. A government could not be sure in advance when it might trigger the excessive deficit procedure, given that most countries technically trigger it anyway because of their starting level of established debt. Further clarification of how far the permitted latitude might be used would be essential for prudent budgetary planning.

So far member states have wrestled with the need under the treaty to cut their budget deficits by a combination of tax increases and spending reductions. The British government, which decided on deficit reduction for a variety of reasons, relied in the early years on tax increases. Subsequently, growth has picked up following the exit from the ERM, allowing the deficit to reduce while spending rises and tax rates are cut. Other European countries have been unable to establish such a virtuous circle. Most continental countries have concentrated on spending cuts. The first big round of French spending cuts led to street protests and union opposition. Some of the proposals were amended as a result and a further round of spending cuts is now necessary. In Germany's case the cuts were very large. Spain is also proceeding with large budget cuts. Italy has imposed a special Euro-tax.

At some point the domestic political consequences of these cuts will clash with the treaty imperative. It is surprising that the electorates have had to put up with so much pain for so long in the name of monetary union. Many political parties on the continent accept it as axiomatic that all else has to suffer in order to qualify under Maastricht. It is amazing that socialist governments and supporters are happy with such large spending cuts, and odd that any type of politician finds the mass unemployment the scheme is creating acceptable.

Those who claim that enough budgetary control would remain in the hands of member states themselves usually point to the fact that a state could still raise both spending and taxation, or lower them, leaving the deficit unchanged. As we shall see in chapter 7, it is quite likely that a country setting out to pursue a policy of low taxation would be blocked. Such a country would anyway have to make a bigger contribution to Community spending to cope with the extra pressures on spending the monetary union would generate.

Member states would be severely constrained in their budgetary policies. If the treaty was strictly enforced most of them would have no leeway and would have to make huge cuts in public spending. If the treaty was not properly enforced they would, at the whim of the Community, be subject to effective budget decisions being taken in Brussels, at the discretion of the Council. Democratic accountability for budget decisions at home would have vanished. Ministers would be left defending tax increases or spending cuts which they had not wanted and probably disagreed with. The strikes and protests in France in 1995 are a sign of things to come.

In the United Kingdom some of the large unions have moved from Euro-enthusiasm to Euro-scepticism on the currency issue, as they now believe that massive budget cuts would be needed to qualify and stay in. They see this as a direct assault on the jobs and livelihood of their members. For those of us who want a smaller state the prospect of this policy is also unappealing, as we see that the cuts would be clumsy, often damaging policies that are needed, while government in total would grow as the European Union built up its own pattern of spending. I do not want Britain to have to sack nurses and teachers in order to pay the salaries of more officials in Brussels.

The Council of Ministers and the Commission would gradually seek more and more to control budgets and deposits. The Central Bank would want to know the totals and timings of member states' borrowings, so as to be able to manage the markets. The message is clear. Abolish the pound, and surrender the UK's right to settle its own budget.

6

Why a single economic policy will not work

The Maastricht Treaty states in Article 102a that they wish to progress to a common economic policy: 'Member states shall conduct their economic policies with a view to contributing to the achievement of the objectives of the Community, as defined in Article 2, and in the context of the broad guidelines referred to in Article 103(2).' Article 2 is an article of principle, stating that economic union is an aim, requiring 'a harmonious and balanced development of economic activities, sustainable and non-inflationary growth respecting the environment, a high degree of convergence of economic performance . . . and economic and social cohesion and solidarity among member states'.

Each member state has a duty to coordinate its economic policies with those of the others. The Council, on a recommendation from the Commission, is charged with the task of agreeing broad guidelines for the economic polices. Member states have to supply regular information about their economic policies and performance to the Commission, who report on it to the Council. If a member state is thought to be following a policy outside the European guidelines, or generally unhelpful to economic and monetary union, the Council decides the policy is inconsistent and may make its conclusions public.

This approach is buttressed by stronger measures in specific economic areas. The original EEC treaties established a customs union, with a common external tariff, and the abolition of most customs duties and quantitative restrictions on trade between member states. It established a common agricultural policy, whose aims included the stabilization of markets and the creation of one market-controlling organization or group of organizations. It included a common fisheries policy, the free movement of persons, capital and services, a common transport policy and common competition and commercial policies.

The Maastricht Treaty takes the creation of a common economic policy a lot further than the earlier treaties. The deliberate establishment of a Community monetary policy and a single currency effectively creates a single economic policy, by having one exchange rate, one interest rate and one set of rules over borrowing for all member states. The Community's interest in member states' economic policies is more relevant for the preparation and transitional phases than it will be after the creation of the single currency; then it will be impossible for countries to follow widely divergent policies, because they will no longer control the main levers of economic policy.

The main test of convergence for economic policies is laid out in the Protocol to the treaty. We have already seen how controlling budget deficits is central to this task. There are two other criteria which are singled out for especial interest and monitoring: the inflation rate and the long-term interest rate.

In order to qualify for monetary union a member state has to achieve 'a high degree of price stability'. The language is different from that applying to the new currency and the new Central Bank which is mandated to achieve price stability. The Protocol defines the requirement very precisely: it is a relative requirement, measured against the performance of other member states. To qualify, a member state has to ensure that its average inflation rate in the year before its application for membership of the single currency is considered is not more than 1.5 per cent above the average of the best three member states.

This wording implies that the Central Bank for Europe does have a tougher policy in mind than the policies currently being pursued, as it aims to achieve price stability, which must mean zero inflation. Low inflation is seen as an essential prerequisite, and rightly so. The shock of going into a single currency run for zero inflation

Table 1   Short-term interest rate differentials

ERM Countries

	Q4 94	Q1 95	Q2 95	Q3 95	Q4 95	Q1 96	Q2 96	Q3 96
Belgium								
Interest rate differentials	0.0	0.7	0.5	0.1	0.1	0.0	0.0	0.0
Exchange rate volatility	0.0	0.1	0.1	0.0	0.0	0.0	0.0	0.0
Interest rate volatility	4.5	15.9	7.2	5.2	3.4	2.7	2.4	2.5
Denmark								
Interest rate differentials	1.0	1.4	2.2	1.6	1.3	0.9	0.5	0.5
Exchange rate volatility	0.1	0.3	0.2	0.1	0.1	0.0	0.0	0.0
Interest rate volatility	5.6	18.0	5.5	5.2	6.2	4.9	3.7	3.3
Germany								
Interest rate differentials	–	–	–	–	–	–	–	–
Exchange rate volatility	–	–	–	–	–	–	–	–
Interest rate volatility	2.9	3.1	1.7	1.8	2.1	2.4	1.6	2.3
Spain								
Interest rate differentials	2.7	4.0	4.9	5.2	5.4	5.3	4.2	4.0
Exchange rate volatility	0.1	0.7	0.5	0.3	0.2	0.2	0.2	0.2
Interest rate volatility	3.6	11.6	4.7	2.7	5.3	4.8	4.6	2.9
France								
Interest rate differentials	0.5	1.6	2.9	1.8	2.2	1.1	0.7	0.6
Exchange rate volatility	0.1	0.4	0.4	0.2	0.3	0.1	0.1	0.1
Interest rate volatility	4.7	22.7	13.7	7.8	21.6	6.5	3.4	6.0
Ireland								
Interest rate differentials	0.6	1.5	2.2	1.9	1.7	1.8	1.8	2.4
Exchange rate volatility	0.2	0.6	0.6	0.4	0.4	0.3	0.2	0.3
Interest rate volatility	6.0	15.4	5.7	4.8	4.6	4.5	3.0	4.1
Netherlands								
Interest rate differentials	0.1	0.1	−0.1	−0.3	−0.2	−0.2	−0.4	−0.3
Exchange rate volatility	0.0	0.0	0.0	0.0	0.0	0.0	0.0	0.0
Interest rate volatility	3.2	2.6	2.3	1.7	1.9	2.5	2.5	2.8
Austria								
Interest rate differentials	−0.1	0.0	0.1	0.0	0.2	0.1	0.0	0.2
Exchange rate volatility	0.0	0.0	0.0	0.0	0.0	0.0	0.0	0.0
Interest rate volatility	1.5	1.7	1.1	1.8	3.1	2.8	2.1	1.4

Non-ERM countries

	Q4 94	Q1 95	Q2 95	Q3 95	Q4 95	Q1 96	Q2 96	Q3 96
Portugal								
Interest rate differentials	5.0	5.5	5.9	5.1	5.2	4.8	4.0	4.1
Exchange rate volatility	0.1	0.3	0.2	0.2	0.2	0.1	0.1	0.1
Interest rate volatility	32.9	28.8	19.9	19.2	10.6	7.8	5.9	5.0
Greece								
Interest rate differentials	13.7	13.0	11.9	11.0	11.7	10.9	10.9	10.4
Exchange rate volatility	0.1	0.3	0.2	0.2	0.2	0.2	0.2	0.2
Interest rate volatility	9.6	24.7	8.4	6.5	30.2	7.1	7.3	12.4
Italy								
Interest rate differentials	3.7	4.7	6.2	6.3	6.7	6.6	5.8	5.4
Exchange rate volatility	0.3	1.3	0.8	0.7	0.6	0.5	0.4	0.3
Interest rate volatility	9.5	18.7	9.8	6.8	6.9	9.1	7.5	7.1
Finland								
Interest rate differentials	0.3	0.9	1.4	1.7	1.1	0.8	0.5	0.2
Exchange rate volatility	0.4	0.4	0.3	0.4	0.3	0.3	0.3	0.2
Interest rate volatility	6.5	4.5	3.8	2.9	6.6	4.6	1.4	3.0
Sweden								
Interest rate differentials	2.8	31.3	4.4	4.8	4.8	4.3	2.8	1.9
Exchange rate volatility	0.5	0.8	0.7	0.7	0.6	0.6	0.4	0.4
Interest rate volatility	6.3	6.4	5.0	3.3	3.6	6.7	4.0	2.6
UK								
Interest rate differentials	0.9	1.6	2.1	2.4	2.7	2.8	2.7	2.5
Exchange rate volatility	0.3	0.7	0.7	0.4	0.4	0.3	0.3	0.4
Interest rate volatility	5.4	5.5	7.9	3.3	2.3	3.0	2.6	1.4

A short-term interest rate differential is the difference between interest rates in the given country, and in another one – in this case Germany.

Volatility figures measure how far the exchange rate or interest rate changes over time. A high figure means it is very variable.

would be crippling for an economy used to 5–10 per cent inflation. The tighter money policy would immediately contract the credit available, closing factories and sacrificing jobs. The authors of the treaty clearly assumed that the best three performers would be experiencing inflation of around 1–2 per cent, so that the shock of going from that to 0 per cent would be containable.

The other requirement is the convergence of interest rates. Again the Protocol is very clear. It says that a member state seeking to join has to show that its nominal average interest rates on long-term government bonds were not more than 2 per cent above those of the three lowest inflation countries. Again this is a sensible requirement, even a generous one. Once in the currency union, interest rates should snap into line for all countries. There would be little difference in perceived risk as between the German and French governments, as no country is able under the rules to borrow too much and get into difficulties with repayment. The treaty aim is to make sure that member states do not immediately on entry receive a big bonus for other countries' hard work in getting their long-term interest rates down.

According to most commentators, convergence of interest rates, deficits and inflation rates is all that is required. Yet the treaty has another important clause referring to the exchange rate. Article 109j requires 'the observance of the normal fluctuation margins provided for by the Exchange Rate Mechanism of the European Monetary System, for at least two years, without devaluing against the currency of any other member state.' The Protocol reinforces this message. It says:

The criterion . . . shall mean that a member state has respected the normal fluctuation margins provided for by the Exchange Rate Mechanism of the European Monetary System without severe tensions for at least two years before the examination. In particular, the member state shall not have devalued its currency's bilateral central rate against any other member's currency on its own initiative for the same period.

This too is a pre-eminently sensible requirement for countries contemplating the abolition of their own currencies. If a currency cannot stay in line with the others in the system, it means that the economies are not working happily together. Preventing adjustment through currency realignment by merging the currencies will mean the adjustments take place in more painful ways, by factory closures, bankrupt businesses and lost jobs. We saw this process at work in the last days of the ERM and its narrow bands, before the system fell apart.

The architects of Maastricht have never owned up to the disaster of the ERM. The idea behind the single-currency scheme was to bring the European currencies more and more into line with one another, gradually narrowing the permitted bands of divergence, until one day it could be a small step and a natural transition to having the ecu instead of the individual currencies. This approach was destroyed in September 1992 when sterling and the lira pulled out of the ERM, and many other currencies realigned. Since then there has been no attempt to create a narrow-band ERM. Currencies have been allowed a lot more scope to fluctuate against each other. Under the strict interpretation of what the treaty meant, no country apart from Germany and The Netherlands could meet the currency criterion of the treaty.

Apologists of the treaty argue one of two different cases. Some say that the treaty now means the reformed ERM, allowing 15 per cent rather than 2.25 per cent fluctuation. Any country which can meet this wide and generous limit will be able to qualify under the currency criterion. This is the view of the German central bank, which sees membership of the new ERM as essential to qualify. On this interpretation of the treaty Britain does not have an option to join, as she is not a member of the ERM.

The alternative explanation is that the member states have decided that the treaty has been superseded by events. On this interpretation, favoured by the UK government, the UK could qualify if other member states agreed that the pound had been stable enough outside the ERM, on criteria still to be established.

The problem with this approach is that it is not legal under the treaty, so any aggrieved person or company, if we proceeded on this basis, could take the matter to court. The only sure way for the EC to proceed is to decide what amendments they do want, given the collapse of the narrow-band ERM, and then incorporate them in treaty revisions. The EC is reluctant to do this, as it might trigger further referenda in countries like France, which might prove difficult for the government to win.

Many commentators are worried that the convergence criteria are all about monetary matters, and none are about the real economy. It is theoretically possible for countries with totally different economies to qualify under these terms. For example, a country with half the income per head of the average could so order its monetary affairs as to meet the requirements. Critics wish to see living standards, growth, employment and other crucial matters also taken into account.

This is very unlikely. The architects of the scheme were the French and the Germans. The Germans were particularly influential, and they have always been preoccupied with inflation. This is understandable, given the hyper-inflation in the interwar years – which led to the rise of Hitler. To them, all that matters is a very tough regime to ensure low or no inflation. It is very unlikely that member states would be persuaded to reopen the criteria for entry into a single currency with a view to including a new range of real-economy criteria as well.

Britain can, of course, apply such criteria herself to her own possible entry, given the flexible nature of the opt-out. It is entirely up to Britain to decide whether to seek membership or not. How we do so is up to us. We could, for example, say we will only join if a series of real-economy convergence criteria are met. I am not sure how this might work, given the substantial gap opening up between British and continental performance. For example, it would be sensible to say that any member state joining a common currency area should have a similar level of unemployment to other members joining the area. If members join with very divergent

Table 2 Unemployment rates *(Percentage of the workforce unemployed by country)*

	1994	1995	1996
Belgium	10.0	9.9	9.7
Denmark	12.3	10.3	9.0
Germany	9.6	9.4	10.2
Greece	9.6	10.0	9.8
Spain	24.2	22.9	22.4
France	12.2	11.7	12.7
Ireland	15.0	13.0	11.7
Italy	11.3	12.0	12.1
Luxembourg	2.7	3.0	3.2
Netherlands	6.8	7.0	6.3
Austria	4.4	3.8	4.2
Portugal	6.8	7.2	7.2
Finland	18.4	17.2	16.5
Sweden	8.0	7.7	7.8
UK	9.4	8.3	7.7

levels of unemployment it will require much bigger and dearer regional policies, and it will make the pursuit of a non-inflationary monetary policy more difficult.

For example, Britain might suggest that unemployment should vary between states by no more than 2 per cent. But as British unemployment is much more than 2 per cent lower than German, French or Italian, let alone Spanish, all it would mean is that we would not join the union. We would have no way of making the others lower their unemployment – indeed they would be pledged not to by policies designed to sack more public-sector workers to curb their deficits, and to keep private enterprise constrained by tight money. We would clearly have no interest in increasing our unemployment to qualify, so the proposal would be of no significance. Similarly, any criterion we might like to adopt to ensure convergence of living standards first would not operate. Greece, Portugal and Spain would not accept such a further obstacle

Table 3 Unit labour costs, wages and productivity (*Percentage changes year by year*)

	1991	1992	1993	1994	1995	1996
Belgium						
Nominal unit labour costs	6.3	3.5	3.9	0.5	1.0	0.0
Compensation per employee	8.1	5.9	4.3	4.0	2.6	1.2
Productivity	1.8	2.4	0.4	3.5	1.6	1.2
Denmark						
Nominal unit labour costs	1.9	3.1	−0.7	0.0	2.6	3.1
Compensation per employee	4.3	3.8	1.6	3.6	3.6	3.7
Productivity	2.4	0.7	2.3	3.6	1.0	0.6
Germany						
Nominal unit labour costs	3.3	6.2	3.7	−0.1	1.3	0.4
Compensation per employee	5.9	10.6	4.3	3.4	3.6	2.6
Productivity	2.5	4.4	0.6	3.5	2.3	2.2
Greece						
Nominal unit labour costs	9.3	11.3	10.7	12.3	11.3	8.8
Compensation per employee	15.4	10.2	8.6	11.9	12.5	10.0
Productivity	6.1	−1.1	−2.1	−0.4	1.2	1.2
Spain						
Nominal unit labour costs	7.4	6.8	3.3	1.0	2.0	3.3
Compensation per employee	8.6	9.7	6.5	3.1	2.4	3.7
Productivity	1.2	2.9	3.2	2.1	0.4	0.4
France						
Nominal unit labour costs	4.0	2.8	2.9	0.2	1.2	1.6
Compensation per employee	4.4	4.4	2.3	2.0	1.9	1.9
Productivity	0.4	1.6	−0.6	1.8	0.7	0.3
Ireland						
Nominal unit labour costs	1.6	−5.9	0.0	−6.1	−9.3	−6.2
Compensation per employee	5.6	4.6	5.8	1.6	2.4	3.5
Productivity	4.0	10.5	5.8	7.7	11.7	9.7
Italy						
Nominal unit labour costs	9.0	4.3	2.0	−1.0	2.1	5.2
Compensation per employee	8.8	6.4	4.1	2.9	6.0	5.7
Productivity	−0.2	2.1	2.1	3.9	3.9	0.5

contd	1991	1992	1993	1994	1995	1996
Luxembourg						
Nominal unit labour costs	4.1	5.5	4.6	4.0	3.1	2.6
Compensation per employee	4.5	4.9	5.4	4.2	3.0	2.9
Productivity	0.4	−0.6	0.8	0.2	−0.1	0.3
Netherlands						
Nominal unit labour costs	3.8	4.6	2.2	−5.6	1.2	0.0
Compensation per employee	4.4	4.1	2.7	2.3	2.7	0.7
Productivity	0.6	−0.5	0.5	7.9	1.5	0.7
Austria						
Nominal unit labour costs	5.6	4.5	3.8	0.5	1.9	1.6
Compensation per employee	6.5	5.6	4.2	3.1	3.8	2.8
Productivity	0.9	1.1	0.4	2.6	1.9	1.2
Portugal						
Nominal unit labour costs	15.1	12.9	6.5	3.9	1.7	3.6
Compensation per employee	14.2	13.8	7.4	4.7	4.7	5.7
Productivity	−0.9	0.9	0.9	0.8	3.0	2.1
Finland						
Nominal unit labour costs	8.0	−2.1	−4.6	−2.1	2.3	1.9
Compensation per employee	7.0	1.8	1.2	2.5	4.4	3.4
Productivity	−1.0	3.9	5.8	4.6	2.1	1.5
Sweden						
Nominal unit labour costs	3.9	−3.3	−4.1	2.2	3.5	4.5
Compensation per employee	5.7	3.7	3.7	3.6	3.5	5.8
Productivity	1.8	7.0	7.8	1.4	0.0	1.3
UK						
Nominal unit labour costs	6.3	3.5	1.0	0.0	1.7	2.0
Compensation per employee	8.0	6.1	3.6	3.8	3.4	3.7
Productivity	1.7	2.6	2.6	3.8	1.7	1.7
EU-15						
Nominal unit labour costs	5.7	4.5	2.6	0.0	1.7	2.2
Compensation per employee	7.0	7.2	4.0	3.2	3.7	3.4
Productivity	1.3	2.7	1.4	3.2	2.0	1.2

Nominal unit wage costs are the costs of employing people to make a given amount of output. Compensation per employee is average earnings per worker. Productivity changes measure improvements in efficiency in making goods.

in their way to currency union, and they could veto such a suggestion from Britain.

The scheme is a currency and monetary one. The currency proposals have been all but destroyed by markets, which have judged that the European economies are not ready to be merged. So far the markets have accepted that France and Germany may be determined to go ahead anyway, and they have priced French and German bonds accordingly. There is no likelihood of any common sense emerging to consider the real economy as well as the monetary one, and no prospect of the Mediterranean countries being admitted in the first wave of countries joining. Discussion has already turned in the Community to how the non-members of the union could be disciplined, to prevent them gaining an advantage by having more competitive currencies.

The single economic policy of the treaty is incomplete. It is all about exchange rates, money and inflation; it ignores jobs, incomes and output. If pursued to its conclusion it could easily alienate the voters of Europe, who think jobs and income are more important than financial matters. As a single currency was implemented the participants would find they needed to centralize and harmonize more and more of their economic policies. One currency, one bank, one interest rate would lead inevitably to one budget and one economic policy as politicians struggled to cope with the unruly forces the euro unleashed.

7

Why taxes would have to go up

Exponents of the single currency tell us constantly that tax policy will remain in the hands of member states and national parliaments, even after a single-currency union has been created. We have seen how the treaty requires the new authorities to control deficits and to influence spending priorities. Yet a single currency points ineluctably to higher European public spending and to harmonized taxation, if not to common taxation set by a European Parliament.

The Commission and some member states have already accepted that there will need to be bigger programmes to transfer money around the currency union from the more successful to the less successful areas. The European Community has regional programmes in place. Taxpayers in countries like Germany and the UK pay more into the EC so that poorer countries like Greece and Portugal can draw more out. Many wish to see this expanded, and more money sent on a regional basis from successful regions like the south of England to less successful regions like Eastern Germany or Sicily.

Any currency union has to accept that the common exchange rate, common interest rates and common monetary conditions they create may not be ideal for all parts of them. The larger the currency union area, and the more diverse its parts, the more tension there is in the economic system and the more need there is for palliatives. If unemployment rises too far or too fast in the UK one option available to British governments, and to the market if currencies are floating, is to devalue the pound, making British goods more price competitive. If, on the other hand, British goods are very competitive, markets and the authorities might decide to revalue the pound. We have seen this happening in recent years, with the pound going from $2 down to $1 in the early 1980s, and now revalued to $1.60. The results of the devaluation against continental currencies when we came out of the Exchange Rate Mechanism were especially favourable, ushering in a period of strong growth and good competitiveness for British products: so much so that subsequently the pound has risen against the DM.

This strategy cannot work for individual parts of our currency union if they become uncompetitive within the United Kingdom. The contrast between the two parts of the island of Ireland is instructive. Until the late 1970s the Republic of Ireland and Northern Ireland were both part of the sterling single-currency area. Southern Ireland then decided to split away and create her own currency. The initial devaluation helped her competitiveness against the UK; subsequently her currency rose a bit against the pound sterling. Her economy has done quite well since setting up a separate currency, for that and other reasons. She has enjoyed greater flexibility by being able to change the value of her currency against sterling, helping her trade with by far her largest trading partner. She has also received substantial EC payments. In contrast, Northern Ireland has remained part of the sterling area, as part of her commitment to being part of the UK. She has not been able to devalue against the rest of the UK to become more competitive. The UK government has felt it necessary to put large subsidies into the Northern Irish economy to mitigate the problems of high unemployment.

The same problems can be seen on Merseyside, where there is no problem with terrorist violence. Persistently high unemployment in Liverpool cannot be solved by devaluation, so high levels of subsidy payments and transfers are made.

No one suggests that Liverpool should have a separate currency. In Northern Ireland the majority community want to keep the pound as a symbol of their belonging to the UK; Irish nationalists would like a currency union with Eire. It is a vivid illustration of the strong connection between currency issues and issues of nationhood. People elsewhere in the UK accept an obligation to pay higher taxes and transfer money to Liverpool or Belfast, because we are one country.

A European currency union would have to accept obligations to all parts of the union. If the union included all fifteen countries in their entirety, there would be many regions in need of substantial transfers. The whole of Greece and Portugal, much of Spain, the south of Italy, much of France outside the rich Paris region, Eastern Germany, some of the Celtic parts of the UK, Eire, the rural north of Scandinavia: all would need special treatment. It might well amount to around 100 million people out of the total of 350 million. Immediate plans are to double the regional funds. Aid on the scale of the assistance we give to Northern Ireland or Merseyside would cost much more than that. Aid of only £1,000 a head per year extra to the poorer regions would cost £100bn, and still leave the additional public spending well below the additional levels we give to the poorest parts of our own currency union. Northern Ireland receives more than £2,000 a head.

Unfortunately experience has also shown that regional aid is ineffective at curing deep-seated problems of unemployment and regional imbalance. This is unlikely to deter the politicians, however, who are bound to seek subsidies, and European institutions, as in the past, are likely to give them. The way the official mind works in Europe creates a kind of dependency culture, where people and companies are required to feel grateful for being given some of their own money back, and where there is a great merry-go-round with some winners and some losers. The bureaucracy takes a stiff handling fee on the way.

Extra regional and grant spending of £100bn would mean the UK, given the present pattern of contributions, having to contribute an extra £20bn. That would mean 10 p on income tax, a 50 per cent increase in the Conservatives' proposed 20 p standard rate, as it would not be permitted under the deficit rules to borrow the extra money. It is difficult to see how a currency union could endure for long without large transfers.

There would also be a demand to bring tax rates generally into line. The process began some time ago for indirect taxes. Value Added Tax is an EC tax. The UK had to introduce it as part of our qualification for full membership. The amount of money we and others have to send to pay for the EC is calculated in relation to the amount of money we can raise from VAT. Subsequently the EC issued guidelines on acceptable levels of VAT, to bring rates more or less into line around Europe. Britain has complied by raising its rates to 17.5 per cent, to bring them up to the required levels. The government wanted extra revenue anyway, but the European dimension affected the decision on how to raise taxes.

In a single-currency area it is difficult to believe members would tolerate for long any national administration which decided to set its tax rates at a level a lot lower than the others. It would make that part of the union very attractive to European and other businesses. They would invest there at the expense of the other areas. Jealousy would soon set in. Rules would be developed to require income and corporation taxes within similar bands, just as VAT is now within given bands. The union has already moved to try to stop what it sees as social dumping: one member state having lower cost requirements for health, safety and employment measures, undercutting others. It would be bound to move against 'tax dumping' if one country was markedly more successful than others at keeping spending and taxes low.

The United Kingdom is the country most likely to lose out from any such move. The UK already has a much lower level of income and corporation tax than most countries on the continent, and has kept its overall level of public spending well below that of most European countries. Although it has been a big struggle at home, and although progress in reducing the proportion of national income taken by the state has been both slow and erratic, the struggle has none the less prevented the big surplus in public spending we have seen in the 1980s and 1990s on the continent.

More importantly, the UK has taken some fundamental decisions to limit future growth in our welfare bill, moves that have not been matched on the continent. The UK has encouraged most people to save for their retirement through a second pension scheme. On the continent promissory notes have been issued, saying larger pensions will be paid in the future from tax revenues. The UK has more saved in investments for retirement than the rest of Europe put together. UK policy has also pegged increases in the basic state retirement pension to prices rather than wages, cutting the growth in the cost of that scheme. In the years ahead, as a result of these decisions, there will be a growing gap between the amount of tax British people have to pay and the amount French or German people have to pay if they wish to collect the benefits they have been promised. Naturally British people are worried that there might in a single-currency area be moves to equalize these differences, expecting a bigger contribution to federal revenues from us because we are in a much stronger tax and spending position than the others. That would only be fair, once you have accepted that you owe loyalty to the whole union.

The last thing Europe needs is higher taxes. Taxes are already very high on the continent compared to the levels of the emerging economies of Asia, or the most competitive states in the USA. In a footloose world, where business does not have to establish itself in any particular country or even continent in order to serve a world market, the prizes go to those that keep their tax rates down.

Is there a perfect size for a currency union? Should it be as large as the USA or as small as Switzerland? Does it make sense for countries the size of Latvia to have their own currencies? Was Ireland right to split away from the currency union of the British Isles? I conclude that there is no optimum size, for choosing a currency is not just an economic question, it is also a question of identity, common government and common aspirations. A currency union will only work at all if each person in that union accepts that it is right, and accepts the responsibilities to others that it entails. It has to become an area of common taxation, to pay the bills of regional and local strain within the union.

A recent flurry of speculation has suggested France and Germany are already working on plans for harmonized income tax. They are right to do so, given that they are serious about merging their currencies and economies. One currency will require one budget, one finance minister and one tax policy, as well as one bank, one interest rate and one money policy. The treaty only tells us half the story. The rest would follow.

8

Will we end up paying the old-age pensions for France and Germany?

In recent months the issue of pension costs in the European Community has received a great deal of attention. From the year 2010 onwards the number of the elderly dependent on state pensions will rise markedly. In Germany, Italy and The Netherlands for example the ratio of those aged more than sixty-five to those aged between fifteen and sixty-four is expected to rise from 20 per cent in 1990 to more than 45 per cent in 2030. This will include an increasing proportion of very old people who will need a great deal of more expensive health care as well as pensions. In Germany, Italy, The Netherlands and Sweden the total number of dependants, taking young and old together, will rise to 70 per cent of those of working age by 2030. The Netherlands is expected to see the biggest increase from 19.1 per cent elderly dependent in 1990 to 45.1 per cent in 2030. France sees it almost double from 20.8 per cent to 39.1 per cent and Germany from 21.2 to 40.9 per cent. The United Kingdom has one of the least dramatic increases from 24 to 38.7 per cent.

Unfortunately in countries like France and Germany there is considerable dependence upon state pensions which have not been funded. Conversely in the United Kingdom people look forward to retirement enjoying a second pension for which they and/or their employers have saved. In France and Germany many rely upon state pensions for their livelihood. In France in 1995 public pensions cost 10.6 per cent of GDP. It is estimated that this will rise to 14.3 per cent of GDP by 2040. Similarly in Germany the current level is 11.1 per cent and this is expected to rise to 18.4 per cent by 2040. The Dutch level is anticipated to double from 6 to 12.1 per cent and the Danish level to move from 6.8 to 11.6 per cent. Only the United Kingdom and Ireland have a very different position, thanks to the reliance on pensions for which people are saving. In 1995, only 4.5 per cent of UK GDP was paid in state pensions. This is expected to rise to a mere 5 per cent by 2040. In Ireland the ratio is expected to fall from 3.6 per cent in 1995 to 2.9 per cent in 2040. The European Community concludes

if policies regarding benefits are unchanged and if contribution rates are not adjusted in the future, social security pension contributions would fall far short in most EU countries, implying sizeable public-sector deficits and rising public debt to GDP ratios. In the meantime, real interest rates could increase, which, together with adverse debt dynamics, could trigger a snowball effect of rising debts and interest payments. In the light of these potential burdens, governments are seeking to limit social security pension commitments directly. Reforms have already been introduced in many countries, but in most cases the scale of the problem suggests that more action is needed.

The European Community is right to be alarmed. It portrays here a situation where the pensions burden keeps on rising and where countries instead of resorting to higher taxation to pay the bills decide to resort to borrowing. This would immediately put them outside the terms of the convergence requirements for the single currency and would in the end become self-defeating. If a country keeps on building up its debt it reaches the point where interest payments on the debt become too large a proportion of the state budget and of national income, leading ultimately to the bankruptcy of the state.

The United Kingdom and the Republic of Ireland are in a much stronger position because we have made private pension provision. The combined gross value of United Kingdom pension funds exceeds the value of all the pension funds on the continent of Europe put together. Every month that passes sees more individuals and employers paying contributions into large pension funds. In recent years these have had good investment performances, adding

Table 4a   Projections of elderly dependency ratio 1990–2030
(Population aged 65 and over as percentage of the population aged 15–64)

	1990	2010	2030
Belgium	22.4	25.6	41.1
Denmark	22.7	24.9	37.7
Germany	21.7	30.3	49.2
Greece	21.2	28.8	40.9
Spain	19.8	25.9	41.0
France	20.8	24.6	39.1
Ireland	18.4	18.0	25.3
Italy	21.6	31.2	48.3
Luxembourg	19.9	25.9	44.2
Netherlands	19.1	24.2	45.1
Austria	22.4	27.7	44.0
Portugal	19.5	22.0	33.5
Finland	19.7	24.3	41.1
Sweden	27.6	29.1	39.4
UK	24.0	25.8	38.7
EU	21.4	25.9	40.6

Table 4b   Projections of public pension costs *(as a percentage of GDP)*

	1995	2000	2010	2020	2030	2040
Belgium	10.4	9.7	8.7	10.7	13.9	15.0
Denmark	6.8	6.4	7.6	9.3	10.9	11.6
Germany	11.1	11.5	11.8	12.3	16.5	18.4
Spain	10.0	9.8	10.0	11.3	14.1	16.8
France	10.6	9.8	9.7	11.6	13.5	14.3
Ireland	3.6	2.9	2.6	2.7	2.8	2.9
Italy	13.3	12.6	13.2	15.3	20.3	21.4
Netherlands	6.0	5.7	6.1	8.4	11.2	12.1
Portugal	7.1	6.9	8.1	9.6	13.0	15.2
Finland	10.1	9.5	10.7	15.2	17.8	18.0
Sweden	11.8	11.1	12.4	13.9	15.0	14.9
UK	4.5	4.5	5.2	5.1	5.5	5.0

to the total amount of wealth available to meet future pension obligations. As a result the United Kingdom does not expect its social security payments to spiral out of control in the next century.

If we joined the single currency, it is possible that our relative prudence would lead to us being penalized in a single-currency scheme. It is not true to say that there would be a direct means of taking money out of my or your pension fund and putting it into the pockets of a French or German pensioner. Our pension fund investments are protected by British trust law and we will receive our pension payments come the day of our retirement, assuming the investment managers do well and the funds are properly looked after. However, if we were in a currency union with France and Germany, the fact that their state could not meet the pension expectations of retiring French and German citizens in the next century would affect us as well. Once you join a currency union with others you accept mutual obligations. Those countries that are doing badly will look to the others to make regional, social and other transfer payments available. Conversely, those that are doing well should be in a position to help those who are doing less well. By the second quarter of the next century, if nothing else changes, the state finances of France and Germany will be in a difficult situation. As a result it is all too likely that France and Germany would look to the United Kingdom to make a bigger contribution out of our tax revenues to programmes and policies that would help France and Germany during its period of financial crisis. So while there would be no direct means of taking money out of our pension funds and giving it to French and German pensioners, there would be indirect means through raising taxes in the United Kingdom and transferring the money to France and Germany.

This is exactly what happens at the moment between London and Liverpool in the United Kingdom's sterling currency union. Benefit bills in Liverpool are higher than the tax revenue brought in in Liverpool. Because there is a national system of social security, transfers are made from London taxpayers to the Liverpool benefit office to pay the bills. If Leipzig were in a currency union with London and if they were finding it difficult to meet their pension promises there would need to be a method of transferring money from London.

The Conservative government which came to power in 1979 inherited the State Earnings Related Pension Scheme (SERPS), a pension scheme which topped up the standard state retirement pension. Like the standard state retirement scheme and the schemes in France and Germany, the money collected for the SERPS was not invested or put on one side for future needs but was used for general government expenditure. As a result, pensioners depend upon taxpayers of the future to pay for their pensions payments.

In the middle 1980s the Thatcher administration was persuaded that the State Earnings Related Pension Scheme would prove to be far too costly in the next century. As a result that government took two important courses of action. Firstly, it cut substantially the future benefit entitlements under SERPS, before too many people had committed too much money on the basis of the old prospectus. Secondly, it offered a better financial incentive for people to opt out of SERPS and make their own provision with or without the help of their employer in a properly funded pension scheme of their own. Most people in the United Kingdom now do pay in direct to a pension scheme of their own which amasses savings on their behalf. France and Germany need to undertake a similar type of reform.

If we join a currency union with the countries that have not taken similar precautions we will be asking for trouble. Despite the Thatcher reforms in the field of pensions provision, social security in the United Kingdom has continued to grow dramatically in the 1980s and 1990s. Between 1979/80 and 1995/6 means-tested benefits and payments for sickness and invalidity have grown by almost 5 per cent of GDP at a time when GDP itself has been expanding quite rapidly. Without the pensions reform the whole edifice would soon have become cripplingly expensive and top

Table 5 General government primary balances and interest payments *(as a percentage of GDP)*

| | Primary balances | | | | | |
	1991	1992	1993	1994	1995	1996
Belgium	3.7	3.6	3.3	4.9	5.0	5.2
Denmark	5.3	4.0	3.9	3.6	5.0	5.0
Germany	−0.6	0.4	−0.2	1.0	0.2	−0.2
Greece	−2.1	−0.6	−1.4	2.1	4.0	3.9
Spain	−1.0	0.6	−1.6	−1.2	−1.3	1.0
France	0.9	−0.6	−2.3	−2.0	−1.1	−0.2
Ireland	5.1	4.4	4.0	4.0	3.0	2.9
Italy	0.0	1.9	2.5	1.7	4.1	4.0
Luxembourg	2.3	1.1	2.0	3.1	1.9	1.3
Netherlands	3.3	2.3	3.0	2.5	1.9	3.0
Austria	1.6	2.4	0.2	−0.3	−1.5	0.3
Portugal	1.9	4.2	−0.1	0.0	0.5	0.9
Finland	0.4	−3.2	−3.4	−1.1	0.1	2.5
Sweden	4.0	−2.4	−6.1	−4.0	−1.0	3.6
UK	0.3	−3.4	−4.9	−3.5	−2.1	−0.9
EU-15	0.5	0.2	−0.8	−0.1	0.4	1.1

A primary balance is the gap between tax revenue and public spending, excluding the interest charges on government borrowings. A positive balance means tax revenue exceeds expenditure.

heavy. Even the United Kingdom needs further reforms in its social security system to ensure proper control over public spending and borrowing. How much worse the problem is in all the other EC countries apart from the Republic of Ireland is shown by the social security and pensions figures.

The impact of all this on government debt levels and interest payments is very marked. In the case of Greece, interest payments on government debt alone now amount to 11.9 per cent of total

| | *Interest payments (as a percentage of GDP)* | | | | | |
	1991	1992	1993	1994	1995	1996
Belgium	10.2	10.8	10.8	10.1	9.1	8.5
Denmark	7.4	6.8	7.8	7.1	6.7	6.4
Germany	2.7	3.3	3.3	3.4	3.7	3.8
Greece	9.4	11.7	12.8	14.2	13.1	11.9
Spain	3.9	4.2	5.2	5.1	5.4	5.4
France	3.1	3.2	3.4	3.6	3.7	3.8
Ireland	7.5	6.9	6.5	5.7	5.0	4.5
Italy	10.2	11.4	12.1	10.7	11.2	10.5
Luxembourg	0.4	0.4	0.4	0.4	0.3	0.3
Netherlands	6.2	6.3	6.2	5.9	6.0	5.6
Austria	4.3	4.3	4.3	4.1	4.3	4.5
Portugal	8.6	7.8	6.8	5.8	5.6	4.9
Finland	1.9	2.6	4.6	5.1	5.4	5.9
Sweden	5.1	5.4	6.2	6.8	7.1	7.5
UK	3.0	2.9	2.9	3.3	3.7	3.8
EU-15	4.9	5.3	5.4	5.3	5.4	5.4

To obtain total public borrowing interest payments have to be taken away from the primary balance. So in 1996 Belgium borrowed 3.3 per cent of its national income (5.2 per cent less 8.5 per cent interest).

GDP and in Italy it is 10.5 per cent. Belgium at 8.5 per cent and Sweden at 7.5 per cent also have cripplingly high interest burdens to bear. Given that public spending is around or under half of total national income, it means that in these countries around one fifth of their total public spending is now absorbed in merely paying interest bills on borrowings they have already incurred.

The rake's progress has been dramatic in several countries. Even in prudent countries like France the debt build-up in the 1990s has been colossal. In 1991 French government debt was only 35.8 per cent of GDP and is now 56.4 per cent. Finland has seen it almost treble from 23 per cent in 1991 to 61.3 per cent now and Sweden has seen an increase from 53 to 78.1 per cent. Even the United Kingdom with a relatively low level has seen it grow from 35.7 to 56.3 per cent between 1991 and 1996.

Bankers are right to worry about government debt levels. Politicians are right to worry about the policies required to correct the deficits when economies are performing badly or are in recession. The ultimate solution is to reform social security and pensions in many of the EU countries. This will be a long and painful process. It holds up no immediate prospect of these countries meeting the Maastricht requirements for the single currency but it does hold out a medium- to long-term prospect of better discipline and more economic success. The danger at the moment is that they will take panic measures that are unacceptable politically and do damage economically in their vain pursuit of the Maastricht requirements.

9

Slower growth in the single currency

The biggest argument put forward in favour of the single currency is that it would lead to faster growth. Three main reasons are given: the first is the savings on foreign-exchange transaction costs; the second is the lower nominal interest rates which the low inflation forecast for the single currency would help bring about; the third is the lower real interest rate which exponents of the scheme believe would follow.

Christopher Johnson, in his book *In with the Euro, Out with the Pound*, states that Britain, which has been growing at 1.9 per cent a year since 1979, would, if it joined the single currency, have a chance to raise growth rates to a steady 2¾–3 per cent per annum. An increase in growth rate of one percentage point would be a prize well worth considering, adding greatly to prosperity and employment prospects.

The idea that Britain's interest rate might fall if it were connected more strongly with the German economy is a curious one. Between 1980 and 1994 the long-term real interest rate that Britain was paying for its investment borrowing was a little lower than the German one and 0.8 per cent lower than the French one. When Britain was connected with the Exchange Rate Mechanism it had long-term interest rates of between 9 and 12 per cent nominal. Since leaving the ERM, long-term rates have been around 8 per cent nominal. The pattern of short-term rates has been even more dramatic. In the ERM period rates were between 10 and 15 per cent; in the post-ERM period they have been between 5½ and 6½ per cent. There is no evidence whatsoever that by joining a single

Table 6 Long-term interest rates

	Nominal percentage	Real (inflation-adjusted) percentage
	1980–94 averages	
United States	9.5	4.5
Japan	6.3	4.1
Germany	7.7	4.5
France	11.1	5.1
Italy	14.0	4.1
UK	10.8	4.3
Average	9.9	4.5

currency Britain would automatically enjoy lower interest rates than if it continues to conduct its own monetary policy.

Critics of British monetary policy since the war can point to the fact that there have been times when risks have been taken with inflation, usually resulting in a period of higher interest rates than would otherwise have been needed or would have been desirable in order to choke off the inflation. Far from reducing the risk of this, shadowing the Deutschmark in the late 1980s and entering the ERM in 1990 exacerbated the tendency. Conversely, the periods between 1981 and 1987, and from 1992 to the present day, demonstrate that Britain is capable of conducting a sensible monetary policy and when she does so she can enjoy relatively low interest rates.

Whichever way you look at the figures of growth you have to conclude that the problem that Europe faces is one of a lack of competitiveness, inducing slow growth rates throughout the European Community area. In the five years up to and including 1996, OECD economies as a whole have grown by 10 per cent. The fifteen countries of the European Community have only grown by 7.6 per cent in those five years; the United Kingdom has grown by 10.8 per cent. This good UK performance is despite the fact that 1992 was our last year in the ERM, when high interest rates led to a contraction in the UK economy.

Christopher Johnson shows that Britain's annual average growth rate of 1.9 per cent in the period 1980 to 1994 is almost bang in line with the European Community's 2 per cent per annum and is identical to the French and Italian growth rates over that fourteen-year period. These growth rates are below that in the United States of America, 2.3 per cent, and well below the stunningly good growth rates of the Asian countries. By taking the period 1980 to 1994 British experience is put in the worst possible light, as it includes two major recessions, one at either end of the chosen period; carrying the figures through to 1996 would produce a more favourable comparison.

The proponents of the single-currency scheme are quite right in saying that if the scheme were implemented, and made controlling inflation its prime task, it would create an area of lower nominal interest rates. Germany in the postwar period has enjoyed lower nominal interest rates than Britain or Italy or France because she has been a lower-inflation economy. The problem is that making the control of inflation the sole aim of economic policy could entail very high interest rates in the transitional period and could mean a more depressed economy as a result. There is no convincing evidence one way or the other that you grow faster with low inflation or higher inflation. Switzerland has a good growth record with low inflation. Many of the Asian tigers have excellent growth records with quite high levels of inflation. Japan in her fast-growth era had very variable rates of inflation.

What is less easy to establish is the notion that a low-inflation ecu or euro would not only lower nominal interest rates but would also lower real interest rates. There is no reason why this should follow naturally. Real interest rates are influenced by many economic factors. The economy's potential, the volume of savings, the number of competing uses for those savings and the state of the public finances are all important in settling the long-term rate of

Table 7 Long-term interest rates *(period averages in percentages)*

	1995	Oct. 95 –Sept. 96	Q4 95	Q1 96	Q2 96	Q3 96
Belgium	7.5	6.7	6.9	6.6	6.7	6.6
Denmark	8.3	7.4	7.6	7.3	7.4	7.3
Germany	6.9	6.3	6.3	6.2	6.5	6.3
Greece	17.4	15.1	15.4	14.8	0.0	0.0
Spain	11.3	9.5	10.5	9.7	9.2	8.7
France	7.5	6.6	7.1	6.6	6.5	6.3
Ireland	8.3	7.5	7.7	7.5	7.6	7.4
Italy	12.2	10.3	11.6	10.5	9.9	9.4
Luxembourg	7.6	7.0	7.4	7.0	6.7	6.8
Netherlands	6.9	6.3	6.3	6.2	6.4	6.3
Austria	7.1	6.5	6.7	6.4	6.5	6.4
Portugal	11.5	9.4	10.7	9.5	9.0	8.6
Finland	8.8	7.4	7.6	7.5	7.3	7.1
Sweden	10.2	8.5	9.0	8.6	8.4	8.1
UK	8.3	8.0	7.9	7.9	8.2	8.0
Memo items: EU-15	8.9	7.7	8.2	7.8	7.8	7.5

interest. Postwar European economies have been burdened by high public-sector debts building up too rapidly. Governments have accounted for an unreasonable proportion of the savings flow in the economy, limiting the amount of money available for more productive uses. There has also been a reluctance to save in many Western European economies as a result of high tax rates and the development of a welfare safety net. If people are left with very little at the end of the week or month to spend or save because the government is accounting for such a high proportion of their incomes, and if at the same time the government is making various promises to look after people if their circumstances deteriorate, the savings rate is bound to fall. Conversely, in the more aggressive tiger economies the tax rates are lower, leaving people a higher

	Apr. 96	May 96	June 96	July 96	Aug. 96	Sep. 96
Belgium	6.7	6.7	6.8	6.8	6.6	6.5
Denmark	7.3	7.4	7.5	7.4	7.3	7.2
Germany	6.4	6.5	6.6	6.5	6.3	6.2
Greece	–	–	–	–	–	–
Spain	9.3	9.2	9.1	8.8	8.9	8.4
France	6.5	6.5	6.6	6.4	6.3	6.2
Ireland	7.6	7.5	7.6	7.5	7.4	7.2
Italy	10.3	9.7	9.6	9.4	9.5	9.2
Luxembourg	6.7	6.7	6.8	6.9	6.8	6.8
Netherlands	6.3	6.3	6.5	6.4	6.2	6.1
Austria	6.4	6.5	6.6	6.6	6.4	6.3
Portugal	9.1	9.0	8.9	8.7	8.7	8.3
Finland	7.5	7.4	7.2	7.1	7.2	6.9
Sweden	8.3	8.4	8.3	8.3	8.1	7.8
UK	8.2	8.2	8.2	8.1	8.0	8.0
Memo items: EU-15	7.9	7.8	7.8	7.6	7.6	7.4

proportion of their income to save while fewer promises are made for the welfare net.

Getting down the long-term rate of interest in Western Europe would be a good way of promoting faster growth. In order to do this, governments would have to cut back their requirements for funds and reduce their tax rates, leaving people with more incentive to save and more capacity to save. In the United Kingdom the long-term corporate bond market has almost disappeared, whereas the government long-term bond or gilt market has been hyperactive for many years. This is a symptom of the underlying problem. Most people would like faster economic growth. It makes paying for public services much easier; it also makes it easier to keep the level of taxation down and promotes rising living standards. Much of the British political debate since the war has been about how the growth rate of Britain can be lifted. Politicians of all parties have wished to find the magic ingredient which would transform Britain from a middle performer to a consistently high performer. In the first part of the postwar period people cast envious eyes across the Atlantic to the success of America. As Germany rebuilt herself from the traumas of the war people watched with admiration. It is an irony of British economic development that it was only when the German economy had matured and was encountering its own difficulties of slower growth and rising public spending that the British interest in following the German model became more than academic.

The common thread behind the success of fast-growth economies lies in the attitude towards technological development and entre-preneurship. The climate has to be positive for new ideas to be adopted, for competing companies to arrive and establish them-selves, for savers to be put in touch with investors and for the latent explosive energies of talented people to be unleashed. Too much government is always a bad thing.

In the postwar period a long and riveting experiment was conduc-ted. The Soviet Union and Eastern Europe attempted to operate a totally planned system. Penal tax rates were introduced, labour moved on the order of the government, production was planned in the minutest detail and savings and investments were directed to where the state felt they could secure the most positive advan-tage. This experiment was persevered with whatever the cost to democracy and liberty for some forty years.

Well before the end of the experiment people were clamouring to leave the states that were controlled in this way. The result was a catastrophic failure. Although several countries in Western Europe had gone a long way in the direction of state planning and high taxation, they had preserved enough of the free-enterprise spirit to ensure a much higher rate of growth. Those that taxed least and intervened least grew fastest. By the end of the communist period the communist states were in disarray. Their slow growth meant that their consumers had missed out on a whole new generation of products. Whereas in the West it was typical to have a colour television in the lounge and a modern car in the garage, in the communist states the typical experience was a radio or black and white television broadcasting programmes strictly controlled by the government and a bicycle in front of the flat.

The single-currency Social Chapter and European government scheme does not go to such extremes. The architects of Western European integration genuflect to the idea that private enterprise has a role to play and that some freedoms have to be left to the subject. None the less, there is in the bureaucratic mind an inherent tendency to believe that the state needs to intervene a great deal, that high tax and welfare spending is a necessary part of a 'caring' society and that at the very least government has to be in partnership with free enterprise to ensure fair play and good development.

If we wish to seek the origins of the poor economic growth rate of Western Europe it lies in these very attitudes. There are three million self-employed people in the United Kingdom. This represents a big growth in self-employment in the 1980s and 1990s as a result of the deliberate attempt to create a more favourable climate for enterprise. In Britain tax rates were cut, some of the rules and regulations reduced or removed, and a number of markets opened up so that new businesses could grow. New telephone companies, new bus companies, new water and energy companies have emerged through the liberalization of those former monopolized markets.

None the less, there are still considerable impediments in the way of the self-employed or the small entrepreneur expanding his or her business. Once a small business reaches £47,000 a year of turnover it has to go through the elaborate and complicated process of compulsory registration for VAT. At once, the small businessman is inundated with the myriad of forms and advice and guidance notes, and has to submit regular figures to the VAT inspector. The inspector will then turn up at his premises and go over his systems to make sure that every penny of potential value added tax is being properly accounted for and paid. While a business with a turnover of £100m can handle this within the normal margin of business activity, a business with a turnover of £50,000 and one principal will inevitably have to divert attention away from customers and business development. Many decide it is not worth the hassle and deliberately limit their business size to somewhere just beneath the VAT threshold.

There are also enormous complications in the way of taking on an additional employee. The self-employed man can just about cope with his own annual tax return; as soon as he decides to employ one additional person he has to run a complete pay-as-you-earn system for income tax for that employee and an employer's national insurance system for the same employee. It is another formidable obstacle in the way of entrepreneurs. Their prime interest in life is in the service they provide to the customer, not in the intricacies of the tax and regulatory systems. Many will therefore conclude that it is not worthwhile taking on the second employee.

If Europe is serious about generating more jobs and thereby promoting a higher growth rate, it must tackle these obstacles to the development of small-business success. The European Union seems much more interested in large businesses than small. Bureaucrats like big business because big business can field well-educated people speaking a similar language to the bureaucrats to attend important meetings to discuss new regulations and policy. Very often the bureaucrats and the large companies develop an unholy alliance to defend a particular cartel or monopoly practice against the newcomers, the challengers, the small businesses who wish to compete. Adam Smith stated that when more than one manufacturer meets together they are often planning a conspiracy against the public. It is even truer to say that very often when European bureaucrats, and politicians get together they too are planning some conspiracy against the public. They often do it for the best of motives, but they do it none the less.

In the trade and industry area of European policy they have developed a whole family of directives to control and regulate the design of particular products. Ostensibly, this is to promote a more uniform market and to safeguard health and safety. In practice it can become a way of reinforcing the strong position of the leading businesses in the industry and prevent outsiders from successfully challenging them. In the name of protecting employment the European Community has increased the costs and complexity of employing people. This may offer some temporary assistance to those who are already lucky enough to have jobs but it is very bad news for those seeking jobs, as it reduces the willingness of entrepreneurs to offer any kind of job at all.

Nor is it possible to argue that saving foreign-exchange dealing costs on international trade between member states who join the single currency will of itself provide a great boost to economic activity. Most businesses in the United Kingdom are small. They employ fewer than twenty employees, they sell into a local or regional market and they do not have the time or the capacity to undertake transactions in foreign countries. A typical entrepreneur in Britain is not a fluent French or German speaker. It is not his natural inclination to get on a plane to Paris or Bonn to sell his products when his company has still not penetrated the Birmingham market fully. There is a natural preference for doing business close to home in your own language. As a result, most small businesses are almost entirely dependent on the United Kingdom market for their turnover and for the foreseeable future will grow by widening their product range and their geographical coverage within the United Kingdom. For these businesses there will be no savings whatsoever from the introduction of a single currency as they are not collecting revenues or incurring costs in France or Germany.

At the other end of the spectrum there are very large businesses who already avoid running currency risks when trading between France, Germany and Britain. Sensible businesses use forward markets to eliminate or reduce their currency risk. If, for example, a British business decides to quote for a job in Germany it will calculate the Deutschmark costs and revenues it will incur in order to fulfil the contract. A prudent business adds to its quotation the modest costs of forward cover to make sure it is not exposed on the net position in Deutschmarks in carrying out the contract. Alternatively, the company may discover that the revenues and costs are in balance with only the profit element remaining to repatriate into pounds. In this case the company may well wish to quote in Deutschmarks on an uncovered basis because the costs and revenues will balance out.

The modest costs of the exchange cover at current exchange rates will be small compared with the competitive advantage Britain currently enjoys given the level of the Deutschmark and the competitive value of the pound. In general, British costs are way below German ones, giving British companies an incentive to quote and win business in the German market. The costs of forward cover are tiny compared with the comparative advantage British business currently enjoys.

Most large businesses are global, not European. Even quintessentially European businesses like Unilever and Shell, both businesses with Anglo-Dutch origins, shareholdings and main offices, are now truly global corporations. Both would argue that the dynamic growth in their businesses in the future is going to come in Asia rather than in Europe. Both would accept that much of their trading is going to be dollar based. All oil is traded internationally in dollars. The spot and contract price of oil is settled in dollars, forward and spot markets settle transactions in dollars and many of the costs of setting up oil wells and servicing oil installations are incurred in dollars. If British companies really wished to eliminate the most serious exchange risk, Britain would merge with the dollar bloc rather than the Deutschmark bloc. Volumes of trade on the London foreign exchanges demonstrate that the dollar is still the dominant currency of transaction. The transition from the pound to the euro would expose British businesses to bigger dollar risk as the Deutschmark has performed more strongly against the dollar than has the pound since the War.

The argument for the single currency and the exchange transaction costs comes down to an argument about the advantage to a medium-sized company with strong trading in France and Germany but not in other overseas markets. It would be possible to find examples of such British businesses, but they would be few in number and represent a relatively small share of total British national output. These are the companies who would gain most from the single currency. Medium-sized companies are not so happy at using forward cover and forward markets as larger companies. They have a less sophisticated treasury function. They are exposed to some foreign-exchange risk when trading in both francs and Deutschmarks and they would eliminate that if the national currencies were abolished.

It would not be cost-free for them. While the foreign-exchange dealing cost might amount to 2 per cent for them, taking both spread and commission together, the money transmission cost would often be higher than the foreign-exchange transaction cost. Settling in euros would still require money transmission between Britain, France and Germany, for which the banks would charge. Indeed, it is quite possible that under a unified euro system the banks might decide to increase the transaction charge to compensate in part for their lost foreign-exchange revenues. At the same time the medium-sized business would incur all the transitional costs of re-equipping if collecting money from customers directly and changing accounting systems, invoicing procedures and the like. The idea that cutting foreign-exchange costs should be the decisive argument in favour of a single currency is a very small tail wagging a very large dog. It is attacking costs in the United Kingdom that impact on less than 15 per cent of our GDP. One third of our economy is taken up with foreign trade. A little under one half of this total foreign trade in goods and services is with the European Community. Not all members of the European Community will join the single-currency scheme if one goes ahead, leaving the target turnover subject to foreign-exchange transaction costs with other member states likely to join the single currency at less than £115bn out of our economy of £750bn. Christopher Johnson estimates the possible savings on this activity at £2.5bn. This is an optimistic estimate. In practice the savings, taking account of money transmission costs and the interest charges on the new equipment to tackle the single currency, are likely to be minimal. In a £750bn economy, on Johnson's estimate, there would be a 0.3 per cent improvement from the foreign-exchange savings. Against this has to be set the costs and the lost employment and profits in foreign-exchange dealing and related banking. It is not credible to suggest that saving even as much as £2.5bn in an economy of £750bn will suddenly lift the growth rate from 1.9 to 3 per cent. Lifting the growth rate would require materially lower interest rates. These would have to be allied to a different approach to taxation, public spending and entrepreneurship.

To have a measurable impact on a £750bn economy, policy-makers and chancellors of the exchequer have to be thinking about changing £10bn rather than £2bn. A typical budget in the United Kingdom influences £2–3bn at the margins. Only when a government over a period of years decides to do something more dramatic, as the Conservative government did in the 1980s, cutting the basic rate of income tax from 33 p in the pound to 25 p in the pound, do you start to have some measurable consequence from a policy change. Interest changes can have a more dramatic impact. In a British economy with £1,000bn total public and private debt, every 1 per cent change in the interest rate either adds or subtracts £10bn from the spending power of people, businesses and government. This does not all flow through to increased growth as it is a self-balancing item. A cut in interest rates helps the borrower but impedes the saver. Not all of the change flows through immediately – or at all, as quite a lot of debt has been lent at fixed rates for a long period. None the less, the figures show that an interest-rate change is far more significant than removing foreign-exchange dealing costs or than the normal amounts of money moved around in tax changes in a typical budget.

We have seen the efficacy of lower interest rates in generating employment and growth in the 1980s and 1990s. The long, controlled boom of 1981–7 and the sharper, uncontrolled boom of 1987–9 were both ushered in by relatively low interest rates. The contraction of the early 1990s was brought about by very high interest rates. The encouraging recovery since 1992 has been primarily the product of reducing interest rates by almost two thirds from their peak.

Critics are right to say that the swings in British interest rates have been too violent. In the early 1980s the Conservative government inherited a very inflation-ridden economy and decided on a severe shock through interest rates to reduce inflationary expectations. It did work, but it did considerable damage to many businesses in the process. In the late 1980s and early 1990s, as we have seen, it was the attempt to stabilize the pound against the Deutschmark which destabilized everything else.

Enthusiasts for the single-currency scheme believe that Germany is a repository of non-inflationary virtues and that the German prudence will shine through in the single-currency scheme. There is a suggestion that countries like Britain and Italy, if they were allowed to join, would be free riders on the back of German prudence. We would gain the advantages of the German mantle and German history in the postwar period in return for accepting considerable German guidance over the interest rate and monetary policy being followed.

There are problems with this hopeful prognosis. Firstly, while German postwar experience was indeed an embodiment of rectitude itself, this has broken down in the 1990s. The departure of Herr Poel as governor of the German central bank following a policy disagreement with the Chancellor of the German Republic demonstrated that the bank is ultimately under political control. The same is likely to prove true of currency union. We already see Germany easing monetary policy in an effort to relieve pressures on France. This is not the German central bank's policy but the policy of the Federal Chancellor. Markets will sense that the new German policy is not as strong, as independent and as anti-inflationary as the old German policy.

Secondly, Germany in the postwar period has paid the price of relatively high real interest rates in order to achieve a low inflation out-turn. While it is unlikely that the new European currency would be as strong and as prudently managed as the existing German one, it is quite likely there would be efforts to run a tighter monetary policy than say the United Kingdom has run on average since the war. We could end up getting the worst of both worlds. Markets would sense that the euro was not as good as the Deutschmark, while the euro would end up with higher interest rates on average than we would have had with sterling.

It will be impossible to prove either side right in this complex argument. If there is a euro it will replace member states' currencies. We will then not know what interest rate would have been struck had that member state's currency continued in existence. If the euro scheme fails to materialize we will never know what euro interest rates would have been like to act as a comparison.

The common ground and the common sense in this debate is to look not just at the name of the currency or the institution of the central bank, but at the conditions which are required in any currency to create low and stable inflation and low interest rates. A good rate of growth is partly the result of a successful monetary and interest-rate policy but it is also very helpful in encouraging confidence in a currency and generating the savings necessary to keep interest rates low. In economics nothing succeeds like success. Expectations are most important and there are strong strands of opinion and fashion concerning a country's prowess or lack of prudence.

The United Kingdom is an example of a country which has in recent years been able to change its image in the wider economic world. Although markets are still somewhat distrustful of British monetary policy, understandable enough given the enormities of the run-up to membership of the ERM and of the ERM era itself, markets have changed their view on many other essential characteristics of the British economy. In the 1970s, the United Kingdom was seen as high-cost, strike-ridden, inflexible, a technological backwater. Most of those perceptions have been changed radically in the 1980s and 1990s.

Britain is now seen as the most flexible or one of the most flexible economies of Western Europe, a low-strike country with relatively good industrial relations. It is seen as a centre of technological excellence in many areas and is viewed favourably by industrial and commercial investors from around the world. People also believe that the political risk in the United Kingdom is low. They trust British institutions, as Britain is a rare example of a country that has survived without a civil war or revolution for 350 years. They also believe that whichever democratic party was in control, the broad outlines of policy in favour of a mixed economy and a good free-enterprise sector have now been established. While Conservatives would not agree that there is little or no threat in the Labour Party, many international investors are remarkably relaxed about the thought that the government might change.

These changed perceptions are very helpful in stimulating a higher rate of growth in the United Kingdom. They mean that investors from around the world are more likely to come to Britain than they were twenty years ago. They mean that the large successful liquid London markets are able to marshal money for big British projects or British companies if they wish to develop or expand. Many now see Britain as the least objectionable part of the European Community, inside the walls of fortress Europe but not encumbered with so many manacles and leg irons.

Raising the rate of savings in an economy can best be done by allowing the return to savers to rise. The British government has from time to time intervened to help this happen. It can readily do so by offering more tax breaks to savers. A variety of schemes have been deployed over recent years. The business expansion scheme allowed full tax relief on new, risky equity investments. It has been replaced by the venture capital trusts offering 20 per cent off the cost of any investment for the taxpayer making it. Tax-free savings accounts have been introduced through the TESSA scheme and the general rate of tax on savings has been lowered in line with the lower income-tax rate. The special tax supplement or saving penalty under Labour in the 1970s has also been removed.

Further moves in the direction of deregulating business and cutting the tax rates on business will serve to raise the rate of return further. These are the policy changes that have to be put through if saving is to be encouraged and enterprise flourish. If you ask a small businessman what he would most like for Christmas to encourage the growth of his business, he will rarely say a single currency. He would be very likely to say exemption from VAT registration or an easier way of satisfying the Inland Revenue and the national insurance officials. Some large businesses trading abroad may well say that amongst other things they would like currency stability. If you tell them that the price of currency stability might well be interest-rate instability as we demonstrated during our period in the ERM, they would then politely say no thank you.

It is a deception to suggest to people that if they abolish their national currencies there is a relatively painless way of accelerating the rate of growth by more than 1 per cent per annum and creating prosperity on a scale we have not seen before. All the evidence shows the opposite is more likely. Preparing for monetary union has littered Europe with closed factories, lost jobs and redundancy notices. The crisis of unemployment across the continent is now obvious to all but the senior politicians. The roots of the crisis lie in the very single-currency scheme that is proposed as the solution. Europe has to understand that it is an area of low competitiveness and high costs. It is overburdened with too much government and too much regulation and it is falling further behind the dynamism of the Asian and American economies. Studying Asia would show that it is not a single currency there which has fuelled growth, but relatively low taxation and dynamic enterprise. Hong Kong is a bare rock jutting into the ocean. It has no natural advantages other than the talents of the people who have come to settle there. Singapore is a large city but a small state. It has very little spare land and no natural resources of its own. Yet just like Hong Kong it has shown that it can grow quickly and attain a good standard of living by the talents of its people. These are the countries we should study if we wish to understand the dynamics of growth in the modern world. We should worry that the Asian tigers regularly achieve growth rates two or three times those of the principal European economies. We should worry that the technology of America and Asia is in many fields surpassing the technology of Western Europe. We should learn from Asia and America rather than seeking to shut ourselves off from them.

The contrast between the tax rates in Hong Kong and Singapore on the one hand and those of continental Europe on the other is very stark. In France income tax rises to a top rate of 56.8 per cent and is already at 35 per cent on an income as low as £8,300 per annum. In Germany tax rises to a rate of 53 per cent, which comes into effect at incomes of more than £36,000. Taxes are levied at more than 35 per cent on incomes above £8,500. In Italy a higher tax rate is levied on higher incomes with a 41 per cent tax rate coming into effect on incomes of more than £25,100 and a 34 per cent tax rate on incomes above £12,550. Between a quarter and a third of people's incomes, even on quite low levels of income, are regularly taken by continental European countries in taxation and over half of the incomes of more successful people. In Singapore the top tax rate is only 30 per cent while non-resident individuals are taxed at a flat rate of 27 per cent. Those who work in Singapore for more than sixty days a year but fewer than 183 days a year only pay 15 per cent. An individual in Singapore can earn as much as $150,000 Singapore dollars before his tax rate rises above 24 per cent.

The news is even better in British-controlled Hong Kong. The top rate of tax in Hong Kong is 20 per cent. The tax rate is 2 per cent on the first HK$20,000, 9 per cent on the next HK$30,000 and 17 per cent on the following HK$30,000 of income. Hong Kong's top tax rate is only the same as the UK's lowest rate of income tax and is less than half the top rates of tax in the continental countries.

The position of companies in Singapore and Hong Kong is even more favourable compared to the position of trading enterprises on the continent of Europe. There are no capital gains taxes in Singapore and companies pay a flat rate of tax of only 27 per cent. A large number of sources of financial income only attract a 10 per cent concessionary rate. In Hong Kong the profits tax is levied at a rate of only 16.5 per cent and again there is no capital gains tax. There are also generous depreciation and initial allowances.

It is little wonder that the Singapore and Hong Kong economies have grown between two and four times as quickly as the French, German and Italian economies. The climate for business is heady in these countries. The business can keep most of the profit it makes, often ploughing a lot of it back in new investment and taking on more people. Individuals can keep much more of their income if they work hard. Knowing that however hard you work the state can only take a fifth of your total income in Hong Kong is a great incentive; in France you know that you can only keep a little over two fifths of anything extra that you earn.

The single currency for Western Europe will clearly lead in due course to common taxation. Following the example of VAT the idea will be to start off with guide bands for income taxes, gradually leading to the convergence of rates. The pattern is already emerging quite clearly with the principal Western European countries levying a standard rate of about a third and a higher rate of over a half. While to improve European competitiveness the intention should be to level rates down, the insatiable demands for more money will undoubtedly lead to a levelling up of the tax rates as it has done with VAT. Britain had to bring in VAT in order to comply with European regulations. It was originally brought in at a 10 per cent rate on a limited range of goods and services and later extended, with many more things being brought into the VAT net and with a large increase in the rate to 17.5 per cent. A similar process is likely over income tax. The European Community would also be reluctant to see Britain move ahead and abolish capital gains and inheritance taxes, although this has been pledged by the present Conservative administration. This would move the British tax system more out of line with that of continental Europe and make the tax climate in Britain even more favourable to business, jobs and enterprise.

What would all the money be used for if tax rates are harmonized upwards in the way I am predicting? The European Community will wish to develop a very wide range of policies. It regularly meets to discuss ways of spending other people's money on a more liberal scale. Current plans include the wish to develop a series of European transport networks. In the nineteenth century the United States built large highways and railroads linking the major cities and centres to create a more integrated continent. The European Union wishes to complete a Europe-wide network of highways, to integrate European railways and to build a super-highway of cables and telephone links. Ever distrustful of private enterprise and choice, the European Union would like to carry these out by large state-financed projects. It has put substantial sums of money into strategic crossings and bridge links and is now asking each member state to identify and develop its portion of the international networks required. So far it has been held up for a shortage of European cash; one of its main ambitions is to secure more tax revenue so that it can press ahead with these large Europe-wide networks.

A second source of increased expenditure will come through regional and social-fund activities, granting back to people the money it has collected from them in taxation. Travelling across Western Europe these days shows just how many projects have attracted some money, often quite limited sums of money, from European Community sources. One of the requirements of any grant that any one body or institution may receive is that they should put up a large board prominently displaying the twelve stars logo to demonstrate to European taxpayers that their government is spending their money on ambitious projects. The boards do not point out that European taxpayers have had to send the money to Brussels in the first place in order to pay for these projects. Neither do they point out the extent of the transfers between regions and the magnitude of the handling charge in Brussels for the privilege of getting some of our money back.

In the United Kingdom the main recipient of European regional grants is Northern Ireland. The transfers to Northern Ireland are considerable, but they are dwarfed in scale by the transfer to the Republic of Ireland, which is a heavy net beneficiary. Only Merseyside on the main island of the British Isles has full regional grant status and this is of recent provenance. British taxpayers in the main are sending extra taxation to Brussels in order to provide grants to places like Greece, Portugal and the Republic of Ireland. In a currency union we would be expected to increase our tax contributions to regional funding, as many parts of the union will fall further and further behind, unable to handle the interest-rate and exchange-rate structure that the union as a whole has imposed upon them.

The European Union often pursues policies which make the problems of local and regional dislocation worse. The most obvious example in the United Kingdom is the common fisheries policy. Before joining the European Community in 1973 Britain had a strong domestic fishing industry with protected waters around our coasts which teemed with a good variety of fish. The Devon and Cornish ports, the west Welsh ports, the East Anglian ports, the Scottish ports, the Yorkshire and Lancashire ports were all successful towns and villages. A large number of people were employed and large numbers of trawlers were regularly tied up at the quayside delivering their fish.

As a result of the 1972 treaty the British fishing grounds became in the words of the European Community 'a common resource'. This meant that the fishing grounds had to be open to the trawler fleets of the other countries. The Spaniards have decided that the British fishing grounds are a common resource of great potential and have invested substantial amounts of money in large trawlers with powerful fish-catching equipment suitable for the colder, rougher northern waters around the British Isles. The sudden surge of Spanish vessels into the British fishing grounds has started to denude those fishing grounds of fish. As a result the European Community decided to impose limitations upon the amount of fish that could be caught, limiting net size, ordering the return of small fish to the sea and imposing physical quotas.

Over the years the quota system has been progressively tightened against Britain. Thousands of trawlermen have lost their jobs and hundreds of trawlers have had to be scrapped. Visiting the British fishing ports now is a depressing experience, with few of them surviving and those that do operating fewer vessels.

The scheme developed its own absurdities. Throwing back small fish was done in the name of conservation. The only problem was that by the time the fish were thrown back into the sea they were dead. Far from helping the fishing grounds to replenish it meant that more larger fish had to be caught. It has encouraged a great deal of illegal and illicit fishing and landing, and created a great deal of tension between the British and Spanish fishing fleets.

Under the latest proposals in 1996, Britain is expected to halve her fishing fleet again. Decommissioning targets have been drawn up to scrap vessels and grants will be offered to those who leave the fishing industry. In 2002 the full system will be brought in including special fishing permits. Regulation 101/76 gives the ultimate power to the authorities to control fishing vessels, to decide where the vessel may fish, the amount of fish the vessel may catch, the species, the minimum size or weight of the fish being caught, the type of gear the fishing vessel may use, the number of vessels that can fish in any given area and the amount of time that the vessels can stay at sea.

Already in order to comply with the regulations many British fishing vessels are only able to operate for two or three days a week, while others have to give up fishing before the end of the year in order to stay within the quota limits. The tragedy is that the results of the common fisheries policy are visible in depleted fish stocks and in considerable damage to the sea bed and to the spawning grounds of the fish. Spaniards have done similar damage to Canadian fish stocks, leading to sharp Canadian retaliation in 1994 and 1995.

The decimation of the industry has of course caused problems of unemployment and recession in the fishing towns and villages of the United Kingdom. It is but one all too obvious example of how Community policy can not only damage jobs and employment but also the social and community fabric in the affected areas. Something similar has happened in many steel areas around the Community through the introduction of a quota system and the forced closure of steel-making plants.

Now it is the beef industry's turn to receive some of the same treatment. The beef industry is banned from selling any of its product anywhere in the world apart from the United Kingdom. I have never understood how the Community can believe both that British beef is safe enough for British people to eat but not safe enough for anyone else to eat. If the Community really believes British beef is unsafe they should ban it everywhere. If it doesn't, then it should lift the ban immediately. It is an example of politics interfering in science and a failure on the part of the Community to understand that the British government had already taken action to eradicate the disease based on the available scientific evidence. It is also well known that there are problems in other countries of Europe and yet their beef is not banned.

Policies like these, imposing quotas, limiting businesses' freedom of action, destroying industries by bans will inevitably cause more social and regional problems, and will inevitably boost the demands for more cash to be spent on alleviating the symptoms. The cost of offering money to British farmers to slaughter their cows is prodigious, the cost on both the British national and European budgets all ultimately borne by the British taxpayer. The costs of the fishing vessel retirement scheme and the unemployment payments to the fishermen who are being pushed out of work are also now very large. By these means Europe will not only preserve her high tax levels but will come to need even higher tax levels.

The assertion of governmental or imperial power has always

rested upon the rights to levy taxes, to spend money and to impose the head of the king or other symbol of authority upon the coin. Early British monarchs used their portraits on the coin of the realm to show that they were in charge. In every pocket and purse in the kingdom was the favoured portrait of the ruler. The European Community is following a well-trodden path in wishing to issue and design its own coinage. The power to tax is also fundamental in establishing governmental rights. The British Parliament developed its power by limiting the crown's ability to raise taxes without parliamentary consent. The European authorities are introducing taxation by the back door, using the national governments as their tax collectors. In recent years one of the ironies has been the fact that European rules have insisted upon budget cuts and budget reductions in domestic politics in each country while expanding the European budget. It is this that will lead to ever more common taxation and the harmonization of tax rates at the higher end of the range. It is this above all else which will render the European countries less competitive.

10

Why the City of London has to remain offshore from the euro

One of the most commonly used arguments in favour of the single currency for Britain is the suggestion that for London to maintain her pre-eminence as one of the world's and Europe's leading financial centres, the United Kingdom would have to join in with the euro. Those in favour of a single currency assert that if we did not join the euro the main markets in Western Europe would gravitate to Frankfurt.

This view is encouraged strongly by the French and Germans. They have long since wished to challenge London's pre-eminence as a financial centre in Western Europe. They are also very keen to draw Britain into the single-currency scheme. They regularly argue that if London is excluded from the single-currency scheme then it will be bad news for the London markets. Sometimes it is difficult to understand why they are worried about this, given that one of the main aims of their policy is to try and get business away from London to Frankfurt and Paris. Maybe they protest so strongly about London's interests because they secretly believe that joining the single currency would be bad news for London and would help them fulfil their aim of redirecting business from Britain to France and Germany.

It is quite true that London is the dominant financial centre of Western Europe. Indeed, London is not just a European centre, it is one of the world's big three financial markets. The City of London is pre-eminent worldwide in foreign-exchange dealings. More than two thirds of all foreign-currency dealings worldwide take place through the London markets, making it bigger than New York and Tokyo combined. The same is true of dealings in shares outside the country of origin of the company concerned. London again has a dominant market share, accounting for more business than Tokyo and New York combined. In banking London is no longer so dominant but it is considerably bigger than most European centres and still ranks as one of the important banking centres of the world. More than 500 international banks are congregated in the City of London. The City is famed for the excellence of its banking staff and for the innovatory qualities of its leading bankers. London has a prominent position in the provision of business and financial services, and is a very large investment management centre; it is also famous for its legal and consultancy services, servicing a large worldwide market in the English-speaking world and in all those countries with common-law traditions.

It is important to understand why London has flourished as a financial centre in the postwar period before answering the question, 'What impact would the single currency have upon London one way or another?' In the nineteenth and early twentieth centuries London rose as a large financial centre because it was banker to the Empire. In the early days of industrial capitalism Britain was ahead of her competitors in Europe and in America. She generated substantial surpluses and accounted for a large proportion of world trade. As a result London, Liverpool and Bristol became the centres for shipping, freighting and trade services. London was the pre-eminent centre to finance trade, undertake currency dealings and provide a market in the principal commodities, ranging from gold and silver to soft commodities and industrial products. London's success was based upon the important position of the British economy in the world economy, on the significance of trade within the Empire and on its strong position in transatlantic trade.

What was interesting was that in the post-Second-World-War period British industrial and commercial pre-eminence waned quite rapidly but the importance of London as a financial and business centre did not. British governments seemed to conspire very often against the City of London. Sterling was frequently a weak and vulnerable currency. The government often imposed controls on transactions to and from sterling in an effort to buttress the pound. Britain watched as the almighty dollar conquered the world and then as the German industrial renaissance got under way, strengthening the German economy.

However, the City of London managed to detach itself from the weakness of the rest of the British economy. City experts were able to create a kind of offshore City economy dealing and trading with the rest of the world whatever the weaknesses of the domestic economy or the shortfalls of government economic policy. If world trade and commodities were to be primarily denominated in dollars then London accepted this and became an important dollar centre. If British citizens were prevented from spending large sums of money abroad then the City of London would deal for foreigners who were freer to move money around the world. If British industrial shares were no longer the right place to invest people's money then the City of London would gain expertise at investing people's money in American, Japanese or German shares. If the British economic growth rate was not sufficient then the City of London would make its living by backing the American and Asian economies that were growing so much more rapidly.

In the postwar period Britain benefited from having attracted talent from central Europe during the troubled period of the 1930s and 1940s. It was immigrant talent which founded many of the great merchant banks of twentieth-century London. They found in London a toleration of their attitudes and business practices which they could not find or did not think they would find on the continent, which was being reconstructed from the ruins of the Second World War.

While the City of London often suffered from domestic government economic policies which were far from ideal it did benefit from a long tradition of political and democratic stability, and from a reputation for honesty. It also benefited from governments of all dispositions being prepared to tolerate less strongly regulated business on behalf of foreigners than the regulations they often imposed on domestic activities. Taxation in the 1960s and 1970s rose to a penal 98 per cent on income from savings for nationals but these rates did not apply to foreigners investing their money through London or depending on London's investment management skills.

London also used the contacts and advantages which Empire, Commonwealth and the English language brought with them. London banks and finance houses built important businesses in the former imperial territories like Singapore and in the crown colony of Hong Kong. Through Hong Kong and Singapore they had important investment windows on the dynamic East. Just as British fund managers in the earlier twentieth century had seen the dynamism of the United States and set up investment trusts to exploit these opportunities, so in the postwar world British investment managers saw the dynamism of the Japanese economy early and many made successful investments or built important businesses in the Japanese world. Britain preserved her strong links across the Atlantic. The sterling/dollar rate was an essential part of the Western financial world, with Wall Street and London following each other with great interest.

The surge of inward investment into London in the 1980s added to the strength of London as a financial centre. The decision to deregulate the City, the process which became known as Big Bang, transformed it rapidly. The City had grown up as a club of business people coming from similar backgrounds and sharing common attitudes, probity and honesty in their business dealings. In the 1980s small entrepreneurial businesses owned by groups, partners or directors were transformed by massive injections of foreign capital and a large number of takeovers. The City moved on from being a self-regulating group of highly competitive small businesses to being a market dominated by very large and sophisticated international banks and investment houses bringing foreign capital to add to the native talent recruited in Britain.

The City managed to get through these changes in reasonable

shape. British and foreign talent found that by working together they could make an even bigger impact. The City preserved its excellence as an innovator, launching many of the new financial ideas which generated large amounts of revenue in the 1980s and 1990s. It was in the City of London that privatization first took off, and that many of the new-style zero-coupon, drop-lock and index-linked bonds were pioneered. It was in the City of London that the Eurobond market operated and that many of the financial futures instruments were first tailored, alongside those of their American competitors.

The thesis that all this would be jeopardized if Britain did not abolish the pound is a difficult one to understand. London has grown up because of its history, because of the talents of the people involved and because its cost structure is favourable against the revenues its talents can command. It is not held back by the denomination of domestic business in pounds, even though the pound is now a comparatively small currency compared with the range and reach of the dollar and the yen. The City of London trades primarily in dollars. Converting the domestic currency base from the pound to the euro would make no difference to the fact that London, if it remains successful, would be primarily a series of dollar-driven markets.

The theorists who favour monetary union suggest that the most important type of business that London currently transacts is government business, and that this government business would naturally gravitate to the centres handling euro business rather than sterling business. If France and Germany went ahead and adopted the euro and Britain kept the pound it is difficult to see why this would make a big impact upon the relative strengths of the Frankfurt, Paris and London markets. Assuming the rules of competition still applied, people in Paris and Frankfurt would be likely to find the dealing abilities and terms of dealing in London sufficiently attractive to transact quite a lot of their euro business through London, just as at the moment they transact their Deutschmark and French franc business through London. British government business would still be conducted through London in sterling.

If on the other hand Britain abolished the pound, then sterling government business would be replaced by euro government business but could still be transacted in London. The business which is currently conducted by the British banking system and the Bank of England would then fall to be conducted under the instructions not of the Bank of England but of the Frankfurt Central Bank. In these circumstances, London might have to fight a little bit harder to preserve its role in central banking transactions but again, if the costs were similar, there would be no reason why London could not keep the business.

The argument seems to come down to the threat of protectionism. This has been made explicit when it comes to the settlement system. The European Community is working out a new settlement system for transactions in euros. Some have threatened that unless Britain becomes part of the single-currency system, London could not be involved in the business of settling in euros. This is a most extraordinary protectionist idea, barring a member country of the European Community from settling in one of the currencies within the European Community. It would be quite without precedent and a major constraint on trade, in violation of the pro-trade and pro-competition clauses of the Treaty of Rome. Clarification of the position has shown that of course London could use the settlement system, although there is still some argument about the lending facilities.

Anything short of such a blatant and illegal move is unlikely to succeed in damaging the business of the City of London. If London can offer more attractive dealing rates and facilities in euros than Frankfurt or Paris can, then it will continue to command a decent level of business. The issue of which currency happens to be the chosen currency of the United Kingdom is scarcely relevant to the success or failure of a world trading and financial centre on the scale of London.

If we look at the impact of the single currency on different segments of London's business the pattern becomes much clearer. In the case of foreign-exchange transactions, abolishing the pound, franc and Deutschmark would indeed be marginally disadvantageous to the City of London. If all three of these currencies were replaced by the euro then the foreign-exchange business between them would cease. Fortunately for the City of London most of its business is switching between the European currencies, the dollar and the yen. London would still be an important centre in foreign exchange, whether or not the euro was formed and whether or not Britain formed part of it, but clearly London's best business interests in foreign exchange lie in no country joining the euro at all.

Investment management business would be little disturbed by the decision either to join or not to join the euro. London is a massive international investment management centre with a large range of assets and clients from Asia and America as well as from Europe. Whether the shares of French and German companies are denominated in euros or Deutschmarks and francs makes little difference to this business. If British shares were denominated in euros rather than pounds that too would be a matter of indifference to the investment managers, although their currency judgements would have been eased with respect to French, German and British investments, as there would only be one risk rather than three.

People in financial futures markets would lose, but modestly, from the transition to the euro. New financial futures instruments would soon be generated in euros, and bonds and financial instruments denominated in euros would replace a lot of the lost business in financial future instruments in the individual currencies. However, there would be some modest net loss of business as the degree of complication and the number of cross-rates which need protecting would be reduced.

The impact on business consultancy, legal services and merchant-bank advisory work would be very difficult to discern. London primarily earns its living by advising in common-law and English-speaking areas. This would remain true whether the domestic currency were the pound or the euro. The main takeover markets and the bid and deal merger and acquisition work would also be unaffected by a change in the currency.

The supporters of monetary union concentrate primarily on monetary instruments traded by central banks and governments, rather than on the bulk of private-sector work. Most City revenues are private sector, coming from individuals and companies placing money for investment management in personal equity portfolios and pension funds. Much of it consists of merger and acquisition work, depending upon a thriving market for corporate control, and of raising money for companies; those would go on whatever the currency. In the City, government work consists of raising money through bond issues to finance the activities of governments and some currency transactions in connection with managing the reserves. There would be some loss of business from governments generally if countries joined the euro and stuck to the Maastricht scheme. Deflationary policies would usher in an era of much lower public deficits and in due course a smaller weight of refinancing as government bonds expired and needed to be replaced. There would be an overall loss of business for London and other European markets as a result of less deficit financing, fewer bond issues and a lower general level of private- as well as public-sector economic activity.

Such losses would not be specific to London but would affect all the financial sectors on the continent as well. The issue seems to revolve around whether or not London could maintain a strong position in monetary instruments and monetary control if it either did or did not participate in the Frankfurt Central Bank. As we have seen, it is more likely that London would retain its pre-eminent position in handling British government debt and British monetary instruments if Britain maintains a separate debt financing and monetary system. If Britain abolishes the pound, transfers the foreign-exchange reserves to Frankfurt and follows the policy of the Frankfurt Central Bank, then it will be more difficult for the City of London to retain its pre-eminent position, but if its competitiveness is not impaired then it might be possible.

The difficulty comes in knowing what the regulatory framework would be like for the City of London once sovereignty had passed from the British Parliament and the Bank of England to the officials of the Central Bank in Frankfurt. One of the reasons why Frankfurt has not challenged London successfully in financial services and financial markets lies in the regulatory system which the German central bank has pursued over the German banking system. Some British commentators in the sixties and seventies, when German industrial performance was superior to British industrial performance, blamed our financial system compared with the German one. They felt that a limited number of very large banks pursuing very close relationships with German industrial companies was ideal, and that the failure to do this in Britain accounted for the decline of some British engineering industries. This was not an entirely satisfactory explanation for the big difference in industrial performance. It took no account of the appalling industrial-relations record in the United Kingdom compared with Germany. It did not look at the reasons why British engineering companies especially in the motor industry failed to design the type of products people wanted to buy, whereas at the time the German industry was rather more successful at doing this. But even allowing for some truth in the proposition that the German banks were better for German industry than the British ones were for British industry, the other side of the equation is that the German banks fell further and further behind in offering a wider array of financial services to business and individuals at home and abroad.

Where the German banks built strong equity and loan positions in a limited number of larger German industrial companies, the British banks and financial institutions were servicing the world, offering advice on bids and deals, investment management services, raising money through bond issues and equity financings, organizing placings and funding innovative ways in which traded securities could be used to finance both world trade and world industry. Britain and Britain's financial institutions had to look beyond British shores because British industry did not need enough money and did not know how to use the money productively enough to sustain the appetites of the City of London.

German banks were over-regulated, limiting their scope as innovators and restraining them from becoming financiers to the world. Germany did not develop the breadth, depth and liquidity of the London capital markets and was unable to offer the fine rates and the massive financial support that the London stock and bond markets could offer. Germany was also constrained by state promises to pay large sums of money to people in retirement, whereas in Britain people were encouraged to save for their retirement through large pension funds. Britain soon amassed more in pension funds than the rest of the European countries put together, providing an important pool of liquidity for worldwide investment.

The danger for Britain in joining the single-currency scheme lies primarily in the regulatory approach which the European Central Bank might operate, which could well be against the interest of the City of London. We have already seen moves in this direction through the banking and investment-services directives. Early drafts of the investment-services directive would have made the London system of share trading illegal. The banking directives and investment-services directives are already requiring higher reserve ratios than has been the normal practice in British banks and financial institutions, lowering the return on capital and reducing the flexibility of those institutions. The possibility is that the Frankfurt Central Bank would pursue a very restrictive policy towards financial service innovation and banking liquidity. If the international City fell under this regime, as well as the domestic City committed to the euro, then it could spell disaster for London.

Under a Frankfurt Central Bank and the euro regime the City's best course of action would be to go offshore. It would need to segregate its Asian, American and African business from its European business and make sure that it was outside the regulatory ring of the Frankfurt bank. Continental regulation is stylized by proscription rather than being permissive. To get new products approved often requires a massive amount of paperwork and a long wait. Some of this is already coming into the British system by courtesy of the financial-services directives which we have agreed in the name of a single market.

The question is whether the City of London could go offshore and preserve its flexibility for overseas business if Britain joined the euro. It will require very detailed negotiations with our European partners if we wish to ensure both that Britain joins the single currency and that the City of London is not damaged by involvement in the Frankfurt regulatory system for its offshore activities. It would be possible to enjoy a system whereby London was free to undertake investment management, corporate finance, banking and other financial transactions for countries, business and individuals outside the European Union untrammelled by Frankfurt controls. It is more likely, however, that the architects of the single-currency scheme will see in it a device for extending Frankfurt and European controls over the lucrative business of the City of London which does not involve the European Community.

The European Union could restrict the amount of bank lending the British banks could do on the grounds that it would be part of the general euro liquidity. They could also restrict foreign-currency lending by British banks on the grounds that it might damage their balance sheets and overstretch them, thereby jeopardizing their euro operations as well. Although the European Community is pledged to freedom of capital movement within the European area, it could impose restrictions or capital controls on movements outside the union area. This would be very damaging to the investment management business of London if it came under that particular regulation. There could also be business rules even more oppressive than the current ones, which were drawn up as part of the single-market programme. The Frankfurt bank could prevent certain types of products or investment activity, restrict certain types of investment advice or insist on particular financial requirements and regulations for certain types of financial business.

The essence of the City of London is a competitive international market-place where many new companies and activities are established week by week, jostling alongside the larger and well-established businesses already there. Too much regulation could frighten off the footloose international investors from Asia and America and it could limit the scope for new businesses. It would be all too easy for people in Tokyo or New York or the other Asian and American centres to decide that the regulatory system has become too tight in London or Frankfurt and to direct their businesses to new offshore centres. The biggest threat that the City of London faces is not from Frankfurt or even from Tokyo but from the offshore centres on the islands of the world, especially the insurance and investment management centres in the Bahamas.

The European Community is moving towards the establishment of a second ERM to handle the currencies of those European countries that are not ready for the single currency or not willing to join it in its early days. This would of course give speculators, perhaps including those in the City of London, considerable opportunities to exploit the predictable pattern of government and European Central Bank intervention which a new ERM would present. An exchange-rate mechanism is a speculator's dream. Governments and central banks pledge to buy a currency at a given level and to sell it at another level. They specify the margins and bands in advance, making their intervention as buyers or sellers almost entirely predictable, triggered by a particular level in the market. If, for example, the peseta was outside the first single-currency scheme it would be locked into an ERM against the euro. If ever the peseta fell towards the bottom of its band speculators would know that the European system of central banks would have to start buying pesetas. If ever the peseta was pushing towards the top end of its band the speculators would know that the Spanish Central Bank and the European central banks would have to sell pesetas to try and keep its price down. These predictable events make it relatively easy for speculators to make a good living trading between the margins.

Occasionally a currency comes under too much pressure and speculators then have the opportunity of making a killing out of a realignment. Some judgement is involved in deciding when the rate has become unsustainable and when the central bank buying support is not going to be sufficient. In 1992, when a large number of currencies were at unsustainable levels against the Deutschmark, huge speculative profits were made by all those brave enough to take on the central banking system. These money-making activities would be open to the City of London should the euro and the new ERM go ahead.

For a number of years both Frankfurt and Paris have had plans to wrest pre-eminence away from London to themselves. It has not only been regulation that has stood in their way. Both France and Germany have become high-cost parts of the world. The combination of building costs and staff costs are added to by the burden of high social-security charges and the results of the Social Chapter on Employment Practices. One London-based banker working for a German business told me that when they had been taken over by the German bank they had looked to see if there was anything that they currently did in London which they could transfer to Frankfurt as a token of goodwill. They soon discovered that under German rules staff were not allowed into the office building between 5 p.m. on Friday and 8 a.m. the following Monday; in London people were used to working on deals or investment transactions across the weekend if necessary. The bank immediately decided it could not jeopardize its business by moving to a city where working hours were so restricted. It was a symbol of the difference between the Anglo-Saxon deal-related culture and the more regulated social culture of the continent. Imposing continental controls on London would not sustain the City's pre-eminence. It would undermine it.

PART 3
THE COSTS OF
TRANSITION

11

Is the euro legal?

The treaty signed at Maastricht stated categorically that the single currency to be introduced in the member states was to be the ecu. It is called the ecu throughout the treaty. Article 109g is crystal clear. It states: 'The currency composition of the ecu basket shall not be changed. From the start of the third stage [of monetary union], the value of the ecu shall be irrevocably fixed in accordance with Article 109l(4).' This message is reinforced in Article 109l, where it is stated that each member state shall 'take the other measures necessary for the introduction of the ecu as the single currency in the member state concerned'. The same article says that member states have to adopt conversion rates 'at which their currency shall be irrevocably fixed and at which irrevocably fixed rate the ecu shall be substituted for these currencies, and the ecu will become a currency in its own right. This measure shall by itself not modify the external value of the ecu.' The treaty is full of references to the ecu. Member states now wish to introduce a different currency, to be called the euro. The honest legal way to proceed would be to amend the treaty accordingly.

The main reason the member states have decided to introduce a different currency from the ecu of the treaty is the German worry about selling the whole project to the German people. The problem with the ecu is that it has an established value minute by minute of the trading day, day by day of the trading year. It has been in almost continuous decline against the Deutschmark. This is not surprising, as it is based upon a basket of Western European currencies, many of which are weaker than the Deutschmark or have devalued against the Deutschmark over recent years.

The German people are mainly worried about a resurgence of inflation. They are understandably proud of the strength of the Deutschmark in the post-Second-World-War world. They are adamant that they do not wish the Deutschmark to be replaced by any currency which is weaker than their own national currency: the Deutschmark is a great symbol of the German economic and monetary achievement since 1945. It lays to rest the ghosts of Weimar and the hyper-inflation which Germany experienced in the inter-war years. The ecu is not a satisfactory substitute, as it has been a relatively poor performer.

At German insistence the Community decided that it would substitute a new currency to be called the euro. They then received legal advice that this would be extremely difficult to do without a proper amendment of the treaty. As a result, in typical Community style, they have come up with a compromise which looks in both directions at the same time. For the German audience the Community says the euro is a completely new currency and unlike the ecu it is replacing. Other audiences are told that the euro will come in at the value of one ecu to the euro and it is merely a change of name from the 'generic name' ecu used in the treaty. Maybe the original intention was simply to rename the ecu. The Community then realized that this would neither satisfy the German audience, nor would it quell worries that the new currency would be illegal.

The natural thing would have been to table amendments to the treaty. Treaty changes are being debated in the parallel Inter-Governmental Conference at the same time as progress is being made towards monetary union. The intention is to bring together the treaty amendments at the Amsterdam summit in the middle of 1997, agreeing a new treaty to push ahead European integration. A suitable treaty amendment could be added to include the euro as the new currency, replacing the ecu of the Maastricht Treaty. This would still leave time for ratification of the treaties by the member states and the introduction of the euro on the specified date in 1999.

The Community's reluctance to do this must be born of two

considerations. Firstly, there is the worry that treaty amendments agreed at the Inter-Governmental Conference will need domestic ratification in referenda or by parliamentary process in the member states. Given the difficulty that the Community experienced in gaining French and Danish acceptance to the Maastricht scheme of currency union, the Community must be apprehensive about going through a similar process to ratify a new single-currency scheme on top of the other measures towards more European integration being identified in the Inter-Governmental Conference. After all, in their first referendum the Danish people decided against monetary union and forced their government into obtaining a similar opt-out to the British one before agreeing to the Maastricht enterprise. The second explanation is the worry the Community has about anything which could delay the project further. The first date for monetary union has already been cast aside. Although it would be possible to amend the treaty and ratify it in time for the date now proposed, any further cause of delay is a matter of worry to the principal architects.

Instead of proposing treaty amendments, therefore, the Community has decided upon regulations. They believe they can legalize the euro by regulations under the treaties. At the Dublin summit at the end of 1996 they agreed an Article 235 regulation in an effort to make the euro legal. The second 'whereas' of the Regulation sets out the plan:

whereas it also decided that the name given to the European currency should be the 'Euro'; whereas the specific name 'Euro' will be used instead of the generic term 'ecu' used by the Treaty to refer to the European Currency Union; whereas the Euro is the currency of the member states without a derogation will be divided into 100 sub units with the name 'cent'.

It is an interesting idea that a regulation passed by fifteen member states under a treaty which says something different can be a sufficient legal reassurance to underwrite the compulsory conversion of all ecu and member-state currency obligations and assets into euros. Subsequent parts of the draft Regulation indicate that Community lawyers themselves realize that a considerable sleight of hand is involved in this manoeuvre. The sixth 'whereas' of the Regulation shows the lawyers picking a careful course to try and stay as close to the treaty as possible in all other respects save the substitution of euro for ecu:

6. Whereas the ecu as referred to in Article 109g of the treaty and as defined in Council Regulation (EC) No. 3320/94 will cease to be defined as a basket of component currencies on the 1st January 1999 and the euro will become a currency in its own right; whereas the decision of the Council regarding the adoption of the conversion rate shall not by itself modify the external value of the ecu; whereas this means that one ecu in its composition as a basket of component currencies will become one euro; whereas Council Regulation (EC) No. 3320/94 therefore becomes obsolete and should be repealed; whereas for references in legal instruments to the ecu under private law, parties shall be presumed to have agreed to refer to the ecu as referred to in Article 109g of the treaty and as defined in Council Regulation (EC) No. 3320/94; whereas the provisions of continuity can only fulfil their objective to provide legal certainty to the markets if they enter into force as soon as possible.

This breathtaking and all-embracing provision shows the legal doubts. The lawyers have decided that the treaty must be respected in several important ways. The external value of the ecu must not be modified. To stay as close as possible to the treaty the euro must be introduced at the initial value of one euro to one ecu. It is presumed that contracts including ecus follow the standard regulation of the ecu, although subsequent redrafting has admitted that private parties may have had a different ecu in mind and that private contracts should be respected. The neuroses of the drafters are also revealed by their untimely haste in wishing to abolish the Council Regulation which sets out the definition and composition of the ecu. They are very worried that people will continue to calculate the ecu and to provide a shadow market in ecus after they had compulsorily converted it into euros.

The heart of the problem is addressed in the subsequent two 'whereas' clauses. Clause 7 states:

whereas it is a generally accepted principle of law that the continuity of legal instruments is not affected by the introduction of a new currency; whereas the principle of freedom of contract has to be respected; whereas in order to reinforce legal certainty and clarity it is appropriate explicitly to confirm that the principle of continuity of legal instruments and in particular of contracts shall apply between the former national currencies and the euro and between the ecu as referred to in Article 109g of the treaty and as defined in Council Regulation (EC) No. 3320/94 and the euro.

Two different principles are put in conflict in this recital. The Community wishes to establish the principle that contracts and legal instruments can continue unaffected by the switch from ecu to euro. The Community also has to recognize that individuals and companies have entered contracts on a different basis and may not wish to see their freely entertained contracts compulsorily renegotiated by Regulation or treaty. The conflict is not entirely resolved, with lawyers in the Community recognizing that there may be circumstances in which a private contract will take precedence over the compulsory conversion and the compulsory abolition of the ecu and its method of calculation.

Even worse follows in Recital 8. This states: 'whereas the explicit confirmation of the principle of continuity will also contribute to the recognition of continuity of contracts in the jurisdiction of third countries'. The Community has been forced to recognize that while a regulation directly acting in the fifteen member states can create a legal framework within Western Europe a European Community regulation has no legal impact whatsoever outside the jurisdiction of the fifteen countries concerned.

The spectre of endless lawsuits looms large in discussions of the euro. An investor in the United States of America who has bought an ecu bond may think they would lose out by its compulsory conversion to a euro bond. They might bring an action in a

US court claiming damages for their alleged loss through the compulsory conversion. Alternatively, if the euro turns out to be a harder currency than the ecu and therefore a better bet from the investor's point of view, someone in Asia with an ecu mortgage or loan obligation might bring an action in an Asian court objecting to having to repay his loan in euros rather than ecus. One or other of these people would have a good case to say they had lost out through the compulsory conversion of the ecu to the euro. Nor would court cases necessarily be limited to those upset by the change from the ecu to euro, although it might be thought that they would have the best case because they had presumably bought or invested in the ecu on the basis that it was to become the single currency of Western Europe; there could also be court cases from current holders of Community currency assets and liabilities.

It would be possible, for example, for someone owing Deutschmarks to claim that they had incurred the liability in the belief that the Deutschmark would be compulsorily converted into the ecu and that they had lost out through its compulsory conversion into a harder currency, the euro. Alternatively, an investor in Deutschmark bonds might believe that the euro had turned out to be a weaker currency than the ecu and certainly than the Deutschmark, and bring a court action against the compulsory conversion of his Deutschmark asset.

The Bank of England has understandably been most worried about these issues. Being the voice of the City of London and therefore the voice of a large number of financial businesses, the bank has drawn attention to the difficulties of guaranteeing the continuity of contract around the world's markets. A City of London Joint Working Group has been formed. The Financial Law Panel has established a working group of commercial lawyers to look at the detail of the impact of the introduction of the euro; it is working with organizations in New York, Tokyo, Singapore, Hong Kong and Switzerland to see what legal difficulties are likely to arise in each of those centres. Their initial conclusion is that, at the very least, it will require legislation in the New York State legislature in order to tackle any threats to the continuity of contracts in the United States posed by the introduction of the euro.

This preliminary finding is worrying. If it is going to take legislation in the New York legislature surely it would take legislation in all the states of the United States in order to regularize the position. Otherwise someone will be able to bring a court action in a state other than New York and draw attention to the fact that it took separate legislation to legalize the position in New York State itself. Similar problems could arise in other jurisdictions around the world.

It would be a great worry if the euro were introduced without a proper legal base having been established. The birth of the new currency will be painful and difficult anyway. The pain will be greatly intensified if the first result is a whole series of expensive lawsuits around the world alleging actual or possible loss and alleging insufficient attention to the need to legalize this compulsory conversion.

The Regulation itself contains a fundamental conflict without reconciling it. Article 2 of the Regulation clearly converts every legal instrument in ecus to one in euros. But the third Article states equally clearly: 'the introduction of the euro should not have the effect of altering any term of the legal instrument or of discharging or excusing performance under any legal instrument, nor give a party the right unilaterally to alter or terminate a legal instrument. This provision is subject to anything which parties may have agreed.' The Community is struggling with the two fundamental principles but failing to reconcile them. It has to leave open the possibility that people would prefer to soldier on with contracts in ecus and with their own definition of how a new ecu would be calculated. Although an attempt to keep the ecu going in an era in which some member states had joined the single currency would involve a change, it could still be done. In place of the member states' currencies that had been abolished the person doing the calculation would put in the euro in a similar weighting, leaving in the other non-participating currencies in their normal weights.

Article 3 cannot be delivered. Of course the introduction of the euro alters the terms of a large number of legal contracts. Many of the legal contracts it alters were drawn up before anyone seriously believed the Deutschmark or the French franc would be abolished. Others were drawn up in ecus in the belief that that would become the single currency of Western Europe.

To buttress the legal position the Council has also proposed a regulation under Article 109l(4) of the treaty when the single currency is set up. This draft Regulation attempts to deal with the problems of rounding the denomination of the units of the new currency and the question of how debt and investments would be redenominated. The draft Regulation suggests the need for another Council regulation to state how rounding up and down will take place.

Most difficult of all is the question of the redenomination of debt. If someone owns £100,000 of government securities and the pound is compulsorily converted into the euro they would expect back 125,000 euros if the exchange rate were one euro to 80 p. The gilt-edged securities market therefore needs redenominating in euros if the pound is abolished. The draft Regulation permits or encourages member states to do this without laying down a strict timetable or controlling the process. Article 8 states 'each participating member state may take measures which may be necessary in order to: redenominate in the euro unit outstanding debt denominated in national currency units; this provision shall apply to bonds and securitized debt to allow organized markets to change the unit of account of their operating procedures from a national currency unit to the Euro unit'.

The Joint Working Group has decided in favour of the compulsory redenomination of all government securities in Britain in euros if Britain joins the currency scheme. This would be the best option, given that the change has to be made at some point and given the need for a good liquid market in euro-denominated securities from day one. Similar decisions should be made in other countries that are definitely going to participate in the single-currency scheme.

Doing this will be a very expensive process. It will mean contacting every holder of government securities and other debt instruments throughout the participating area of the single currency. They will need advising of the compulsory redenomination of their assets or liabilities. Where paper certificates are issued new certificates will have to be issued to every holder; where computerized systems are used the computer systems will need updating. There is still no decision on what will happen to ordinary shareholders. United Kingdom ordinary shares are usually denominated in 50 p or £1 units. Are these to be compulsorily converted to odd numbers of euros and cents? Will that require reissuing completely new share certification to all holders of ordinary shares? Is it possible to carry on with certificates and shareholdings denominated in pounds, on the assumption that they really mean euros and cents rather than the stated amounts of pounds or pence?

The most likely outcome of such change would be a massively expensive process of compulsorily converting and issuing new pieces of paper to advise people of their new entitlements and/or to issue new stock certificates.

Legalizing the euro will be a massively difficult task. The documents so far presented to the Council of Ministers do not measure up to its magnitude or complexity. The draft Regulation under Article 235 would do the job in the member states of the Community. However, the position outside European jurisdiction is very different. It is more than likely that court cases will be brought in America and Asia by the owners of Deutschmark, franc or ecu assets, or by those who owe money in those currencies, drawing attention to the discrepancy between the intention of the treaty and the intention of the European Regulation. If the Community proceeds to encourage legislation in some of those overseas jurisdictions, this will simply underline the difficulties.

So what should the Community do? The Community should amend the treaty properly. It should hold discussions with jurisdictions overseas, having amended the treaty with a view to securing their consent to the enforcement of the compulsory conversion of contracts in their jurisdictions. It should understand that this is a vastly complicated and expensive business full of legal hazard. So far the Community has shown itself to be dilettante and amateur in its approach to the legalization of the euro.

12

The Stability Pact

The run-up to the 1996 Dublin Council was dominated by discussions of stability. While the Maastricht Treaty mentioned the need for stability and reasonable economic convergence before countries could join a single currency, the Germans felt it did not go far enough. They therefore presented a proposal for a 'Stability Pact for Europe', to guarantee budget discipline in the run-up to and following the completion of monetary union.

Where the treaty said that countries should not borrow more than 3 per cent of their gross national income in any given year, the Stability Pact decided that member states should pursue the objective of budgetary balance across the cycle. In this way they would be unlikely ever to need to borrow more than 3 per cent of GDP, even in a recession. In boom time, states would be borrowing nothing or repaying debt. To avoid excessive deficits the Commission proposed a preventive early-warning system for identifying and correcting budgetary slippages before they got out of control. Member states were to be fined if they had none the less broken the rules and allowed an excessive deficit to build up.

To increase budgetary surveillance the Commission brought forward a regulation under Article 103(5) to provide an early-warning system. Member states would have to submit 'Stability Programmes' setting out national medium-term budgetary objectives. If the Commission did not like the budgetary plans put forward it could issue a warning. The Council would then recommend that the member states should take corrective action to avoid any possible future breach of the 3 per cent ceiling.

The proposed Council Regulation on the strengthening of the

surveillance and coordination of budgetary positions is designed to bite on those member states which join the single currency. Recital 4 says that having a reference value of 3 per cent of GDP for government borrowing is not sufficient in itself and adds the requirement that government budgets in the medium term 'should aim for positions close to balance or in surplus'.

Recital 5 shows the ambitions of the Commission to move in to control many more aspects of economic policy in each member state: 'whereas the multilateral surveillance procedure of Article 103(3 and 4) should be developed to provide an early warning system, in which the Council would alert a member state to the need to take corrective action to prevent a government deficit becoming excessive; whereas this multilateral surveillance procedure should continue to monitor the full range of economic developments in each of the member states and in the Community as well as the consistency of economic policies with broad guidelines referred to in Article 103(2)'. This illustrates how the Commission fully understands that in order to control deficits the Commission will need to move in to monitor the economy very closely over its whole range of activities. Each member state in the single currency will be required to set out a Stability Programme and to update it regularly.

Recital 13 states 'whereas it will also be necessary to make similar rules covering the programmes and surveillance of the other member states'. It was this particular recital which caused most problems when the draft regulations for the single currency came before the British Parliament for debate and scrutiny in the winter of 1996. The government originally decided that these could be debated upstairs in committee. Parliamentary convention is quite clear. While most European documents are considered in committee, when documents are considered that have particular importance or significance they should be debated on the floor of the House itself. The government ignored the select committee's advice that these were significant documents worthy of a proper debate in the main chamber. A row ensued, resulting in the government having to concede not only committee examination of the documents but also a full-scale two-day debate on Europe covering these and other matters.

It was Recital 13 of this particular regulation that caused most trouble. The Regulation envisages a situation where economic policy passes from the control of the member state joining the single currency to a combination of the Central Bank, the European Council and the Commission. A member state under the Regulation has to present full budgetary and economic plans, and these plans may be debated in full by both the Commission and the Council.

The government protested that these matters would only apply to the United Kingdom if we joined the single currency. Recital 13 implies that similar rules giving the Commission and the Council of Ministers power or sway over economic policy are to be brought forward to govern even those states which do not join the single currency.

The Regulation sets out what is expected of each member state when it submits its Stability Programme. In Article 1 it states that the Stability Programme shall contain '(a) medium-term objective and adjustment path for the government surplus/deficit as a ratio to GDP; expected path for the government debt ratio, (b) main assumptions about expected economic developments such as real GDP growth, employment/unemployment, inflation, and other important economic variables, (c) description of budgetary measures being taken to achieve the objectives of the programme, (d) commitment to take additional measures when necessary to prevent slippage from targets'. The information has to be supplied on an annual basis and cover the current and the preceding year and the following three years.

Armed with this information of five years of economic activity the Commission can come to an assessment on whether the programme is sufficiently realistic to produce the right kind of budget deficit. In order to do this of course the Commission will have to examine and if necessary challenge the member states' assumptions about inflation, growth, employment, productivity and the like. It is an extremely wide-ranging brief giving the Commission the right to rove over every element of economic policy-making. The fact that the Commission can only bear down on the country with a budget deficit is neither here nor there. The Commission prepares a report for the Council. In Article 3 it states 'the Council, on a recommendation from the Commission after consulting the Committee provided for in Article 109c, may endorse the Stability Programme. Where the Council considers that the objectives and contents of a programme should be strengthened, the Council, as provided for by Article 103(4), shall in general make a recommendation to the member state concerned to adjust its programme.'

This regulation gives the Council the power to approve or to recommend the amendment of the budgets and economic policies of the member states. Of course the Council must have this power. If a single currency system is to have any chance of working there must be confidence amongst all the members that no one is trying to free-ride at the expense of the others. The Regulation gives the Council the power to make a recommendation and the power to make that recommendation public. The intention is that public debate and democratic pressure in the member state concerned would provide the necessary impetus for reform. The fact that these matters come under a Community Regulation also means that they could be referred to the European Court of Justice. The European Court of Justice might well interpret Article 4 in a centralizing way. In Article 4 it is stated, 'in the event that in subsequent monitoring the divergence from the medium-term objective (or the adjustment path towards it) is seen to persist or worsen, the Council shall in general make a recommendation to the member state concerned to take specific corrective action'. This matter could be the subject of a European Court judgement against the member state insisting that the corrective action be taken; fines could be imposed by the court for failure to comply. Throughout the debates in the United Kingdom it was stated that no fines could be imposed under this regulation and that it should not be confused with the fines in the Excessive Deficit Procedure Regulation. It does, however, make the general economic policy of a member state a matter which can be litigated under the European Court of Justice rules, and the court has the power to fine member states for failure to comply with European treaties and regulations. A recent tariff indicates that the UK can be fined up to £3m a week for each offence, payable for as long as it takes to remedy the offence.

It is quite true that if Britain does not join the single currency, under the words as at present negotiated, this regulation should not apply to the United Kingdom. However, Recital 13 makes it clear that similar regulations will be brought forward for member states not joining the single currency. A thousand years of English history establishing the sovereignty of Parliament over every economic policy would be consigned to the dustbin were we to agree to such a regulation.

The second part of the Stability Pact is the Council Regulation on speeding up and clarifying the implementation of the excessive deficit procedure.

The Regulation proposes that the Council will decide when an excessive deficit exists in accordance with Article 104c(6) of the treaty, within three months of the information becoming available to the Community. The Council will issue its recommendations to the member state concerned at the same time that it declares the deficit to be excessive. Article 1 also allows some let-out. It states 'the excess of a government deficit over the reference value should be considered exceptional and temporary, in accordance with Article 104c(2a) second indent, when resulting from an unusual event outside the control of the relevant member state and which has a major impact on the financial position of the general government, or when resulting from a severe economic downturn, in particular in the case of significantly negative annual real growth'.

The Community was split over the tightening of the excessive deficits procedure. The Germans were insistent that the rules should be tough, that they should be enforced automatically by the Commission under the Regulation and that they should result in penalties being imposed on the delinquent member state. The French government argued that the decision should be made by the Council, not by the Commission circumscribed by the Regulation; they believed there were often mitigating circumstances and that each deficit needed to be looked at on its merits.

Many member states have been running large deficits in the early 1990s because they have very high levels of unemployment and their economies have been performing badly. As unemployment rises, state expenditure on benefits increases and the amount of tax revenue coming in from income tax and spending taxes diminishes. If clumsy attempts are made to adjust the budget by cutting public spending in the middle of the recession the problem can be intensified. If the expenditure cuts result in public-sector workers being thrown out of work, they too may become dependent on benefit, and the balance of state revenue to expenditure will take a further turn for the worse. Deficit-chasing public spending cuts became a feature of the Maastricht regime. Country after country was forced into taking tough action on its public spending to try and grapple with the excessive deficits, only to discover that poor economic performance made the position worse whatever it was doing.

The Commission proposal to deal with this problem was that a special deposit should be levied upon the member state with an excessive deficit as an encouragement to them to take more action to sort the deficit out. Section 2 of the draft Regulation set out the sanctions. Article 7 states 'whenever the Council decides to apply sanctions to a member state in accordance with Article 104c(11), a non-interest-bearing deposit would, as a rule, be required'. Article 8 goes on to spell out the detail:

when the excessive deficit results from non-compliance with the criterion relating to the government deficit ratio in Article 104c(2a), the amount of the deposit shall comprise of a fixed component equal to 0.2 per cent of GDP, and a variable component equal to one tenth of the difference between the deficit as a percentage of GDP of the year in which such deficit was deemed excessive and the reference value. An upper limit of 0.5 per cent of GDP is set for the annual amount of deposits.

It is not at first sight obvious how such action would help the delinquent member state. A country finds itself in the middle of an unpleasant recession; it is struggling to control its budget deficit by expenditure cuts, but discovers that the fall in economic activity has been so severe that revenues have been depressed and expenditures boosted against its will. At exactly this point in the cycle it then has to surrender up to half a percentage of its GDP in the form of a non-interest-bearing deposit to the Community. In the depth of the recession in the early 1990s the United Kingdom would have had to deposit £3,000m, or almost 2 p on income tax, with the Community. This would have had to be raised in extra taxes. It would not be permitted for the country to borrow the money necessary to place the non-interest-bearing deposit with the Community, as this would make its deficit and borrowing figures even worse.

Instead of challenging the *principle* of fines, the French decided to challenge the question of how the fines could be imposed. The French and Germans finally agreed that 'an excess of a government deficit over the 3 per cent reference value should be considered exceptional when resulting from an unusual event outside the control of the relevant member state and which has a major impact on the financial position of general government, or when resulting from a severe economic downturn'. They defined 'severe economic downturn' as an annual fall of real GDP of at least 2 per cent. The French won some remission from the original automatic German scheme. The Agreement stated: 'when using the leeway which secondary legislation necessarily must leave to them, the Council and the Commission may receive guidance from the European Council, through, for example, a European Council Resolution. Such a Resolution would give strong political guidance to the Commission, the Council and the member states on the implementation of the procedures.' The French had won the right of a majority vote in the Council to determine whether the full rigours of the procedure would take place or not. The Germans fought hard and included the statement that the Council would have to state in writing why it had decided not to act if it did not act in normal circumstances.

Another let-out clause was included in Minute 30 of the Council's Conclusions. This provides that a member state may plead that an annual fall of real GDP of less that 2 per cent is none the less exceptional. Minute 37 attempts to offset this by saying 'in evaluating whether the economic downturn is severe, the member states will as a rule take as a reference point an annual fall in real GDP of at least 0.75 per cent', and also it says that the member states should not invoke this provision unless they are in severe recession.

The result is a huge fudge. The clear, straightforward German system now has introduced a variable political element. The intention is to control excessive deficits. The method chosen is extremely clumsy and may make the problem considerably worse. If a member state does not correct its deficit within a couple of years then the non-interest-bearing deposit is converted into a fine. In addition, the member state has to produce a new non-interest-bearing deposit. In the United Kingdom's case in the early 1990s this would have meant forfeiting the £3,000m non-interest-bearing deposit as a fine and then putting up a new non-interest-bearing deposit until the deficit was finally corrected. These rules would also have hit many other member states in the union in a similar way.

The introduction of a majority vote in the Council would mean that in circumstances where many of the participating member states were in excessive deficit trouble they might well decide to come to each others' aid and overturn the rules of the treaty and the regulation concerning excessive deficits. This could be extremely damaging to the single-currency scheme, as the currency would then experience excessive borrowing. The result would be reduced credibility for the currency and higher interest rates.

What would be a better system? The only system that could really work is political union *preceding* the monetary union. To have a successful single currency you need a single budget. There needs to be one authority controlling the amount of government spending, income and borrowing to make a single currency work with any degree of success. The Community is thrashing around trying to find substitutes for proper political and monetary control. They have hit upon the idea of penalties and fines coupled with public proclamations against the economic policies of the participating member states. A simpler way would have been to say that a given member state can only borrow up to 3 per cent of its gross national product in any given year; if it borrows more than that it will be denied access to the euro markets. In order to borrow additional money at the common interest rate it would need to submit itself to an agreed programme imposed by the other member states. This system would obviate the need for non-interest-bearing deposits and fines, while recognizing the explicitly political nature of the decisions being taken about member states' economies. The Germans might have been reassured that there was an absolute ban on borrowing more than 3 per cent of national income without reference back. The French and others would have been reassured to know that when a country got into trouble, the political nature of the decisions that had to be made was recognized.

The Stability Pact looks as if it will go ahead. No country has challenged the principle of fining, which is the principal weakness of the whole system. No one has explained how imposing a swingeing fine on a country in trouble is going to be easy or is going to make things better. Nor has anyone suggested that the system will be so successful that fines will never be imposed. It is acknowledged that convergence criteria are not just for a single day or a single year in order to gain admission to the club, but are a requirement of continuing membership if the club is to have any chance of success. The Community has embarked upon a course of action which will end up either in chaos or in the Community having to take over most of the important powers of economic policy-making in order to enforce the necessary discipline on the participating member states. To say otherwise is to mislead the public.

The Stability Pact is the economics of the penitentiary. They lock you in, and reduce your rations if you misbehave. Watch out for prison mutinies from member governments.

13

The costs to business

The task of changing over a complete national currency to a new one is enormous. There are 20,000 automated telling machines handling the existing type of paper-currency note in Britain. All of these would need replacing to handle entirely different styles and shapes of note. There are 500,000 point-of-sale terminals in shops around the country that would also need fundamental overhaul or replacement. All accounting and cash settlement systems would need adjusting; in the period of transition they would need to be able to shift from sterling to the euro and back again using the fixed conversion factor. Around the European Community as a whole there are 12 billion banknotes in circulation with another 8 billion in store; all or most of these would need replacing with new ones. The whole of the coinage would need re-minting.

Only once before in recent history has Britain embarked upon a fundamental change in its coinage, when it converted to decimal currency. It was a gargantuan undertaking for retailers and bankers in particular, and it took a while for the public to get used to the new denominations of their coinage. In comparison, converting to the euro will be a far larger operation. In order to smooth the process of decimalization a relatively straightforward system was developed. Firstly, the £1, £5, £10 and higher denomination banknotes continued in circulation with the same designs and same face value. The main unit of account remained £1, which did not alter its value as a result of decimalization. In consequence accounting systems and settlement systems still used the same large unit of account and all banknote-handling machinery remained viable.

The re-minting of the coinage was made easier by continuing to use some coins from the old coinage. Two shillings became ten pence under the new system and the two-shilling or florin coin continued to circulate during a transitional period. The new 10 p coins were minted in the same shape and weight as the two-shilling piece they were replacing. Similarly, the shilling coin became 5 p. The sixpence became 2½ new pence and remained in circulation for several years, although no new 2½ p coins were minted. Certain coins had to be removed from circulation altogether, including the halfpenny, the penny and the threepenny bit.

None the less, it was a large logistical exercise. Enough ½ p, 1 p and 2 p coins had to be made available on D-Day to ensure smooth functioning of the cash system. A massive public-education exercise had to be launched for many months beforehand to try and ease the transition and to give people an understanding of the new values of the coins they would be handling. At the time inflation was quite rapid and there was a strong feeling that decimalization fuelled it. It gave retailers of smaller-priced items the opportunity to round up their prices. People buying smaller items, especially foodstuffs, took some time to adjust to the new values. It was a great relief to most that the pound unit had not changed so that their sense of values for the higher-priced items remained unchanged.

It would be helpful to look at a number of sample businesses to see the problems they will confront when facing the changeover from sterling to the euro. In the case of all businesses serving a local and national market only – the overwhelming majority of British businesses – the changeover is all cost and no benefit. Each of those businesses will have to change their accounting systems, their cash-handling systems and their tills without any savings at all, since they do not switch their money regularly from one currency to another.

In the case of a small shopkeeper the costs will be considerable. If Britain joins a single currency with the leading group, for a period of up to six months in the first half of the year 2002 all

shops in Britain will have to make available facilities to buy goods
in both sterling and euros. In practice this will mean doubling up
the number of tills in the shop to handle two separate sets of
banknotes and coins, because the banknotes and coins will all be
different from each other and because the conversion rate between
the two will be a difficult one (something like 1 euro = 73 p). It is
a legal requirement of the system that for the transitional period
customers can settle in either currency.

Each shop will therefore need a larger working cash balance or
float each day, something approaching double the cash, particularly in the early days before they know the likely pattern of use
between the two currencies. The pattern of use is likely to change
over time as people get more accustomed to the euro.

A storekeeper will also need to re-programme or replace point-of-
sale equipment to handle debit and credit cards denominated in
euros: he will need to price everything in both currencies and
will doubtless also have to help educate the public. It would be
particularly complicated if customers wished to use a mixture of
the two currencies to pay for a given item.

It is for these reasons that the British retailers have come out
strongly against any kind of transitional period at all. However,
the authorities believe the transitional period is essential, both to
acclimatize the public to such a big change in the currency and
in their sense of values, and to smooth the path of issuing such a
huge number of banknotes and coins. The authorities do not believe
they could get enough notes and coins into all the right places for
a single day of entry of the new system. This is a big difference
from the way in which Britain introduced her decimal coinage in
the 1970s.

British retailers are also very worried about beginning the process
of the new euro on 1 or 2 January 2002. The Christmas and New
Year period is one of the busiest retailing periods of the year: it is
complicated by the seasonal holiday closures, the introduction of
the January sales stock and the surge of buyers taking advantage
of the holiday period to do some bargain hunting and shopping.

British retailers would far rather see the introduction of the euro delayed by a month to start on 1 February 2002; in this they have common sense on their side.

The small shopkeeper will have to educate himself into the accounting and taxation consequences of the new currency. On current Commission plans he would have to present euro accounts before the end of the century, and he would need to adjust his own thinking to be able to handle both currencies for a long transitional period. The euro will be in circulation in wholesale markets and for corporate purposes for automated settlements clearing several years before the introduction of the notes and coin for the retail customer.

The vending-machine industry will have an even bigger task than the typical retailer, as they will have to change all their machinery. For the transitional period they too will need alternative machines, or they will run the risk of losing business when people wish to buy one of their products but do not have the right currency. Like retailers, the owners of vending-machines will need to increase their cash floats for a given level of retailing.

Amusement and leisure businesses will have to change all the machinery to handle the euro, and for the transitional period will need to take both currencies. Alternatively, it may be possible to offer cash-changing facilities so that the machinery could operate on one currency, but it would be a cumbersome way of proceeding. None of these businesses will gain any benefit from the enormous expense of re-equipping as none of them have Deutschmark or French-franc business.

All those businesses taking cash from the public in return for goods or services supplied are worried that there will be problems during the transitional period. Difficulty in obtaining the right quantities of cash would place an additional stress and strain on their businesses. It is retailers above all else who have to guarantee the flexibility of the transitional period, offering facilities in both sterling and euros.

The changes for banks and financial businesses are also

enormous. The BAC system of automated clearing to clear credits and debits through the exchange of magnetic data on a three-day cycle needs converting to the euro. So too do the cheque-clearing and credit-clearing systems handling paper transactions and all the settlement systems for credit and debit cards. Decisions have to be made about how credit and debit cards are going to operate in the transitional period. Will people need a new credit card or debit card when they switch over their bank account to euro denomination or will the automatic adjustment be made on the existing card? Will banks be prepared to run systems that balance up people's euro and sterling bank accounts if they decide to have bank accounts in both currencies in the transitional period? Costs of transactions will be greatly increased during the period of dual denomination within both the financial and the retail systems. Decisions have to be taken soon if the deadlines of 1999 and 2002 are to be met. Although 2002 seems a long way away, preparatory work to ensure smooth clearance and the handling of euro settlements from 1999 onwards means decisions and investments being committed this year, 1997. That is why business is keen to know the answer from the politicians as to whether Britain will or will not join the euro in the first wave. The banking system does not need to re-programme and change its cheque, credit- and debit-card clearing systems if we are staying outside the euro.

The United Kingdom already has a real-time settlement system for payments between member banks within the United Kingdom. A typical daily transaction volume of £120bn is handled through this computerized settlement. If Britain decides to join the single currency, then our CHAPS clearing system will need linking to the Target clearing system being proposed for members of the single currency in the European Community. Our own real-time settlement system is influencing the design and structure of the new euro Target system. Discussions at the moment cover matters like whether there should be a common price for settlement within Target whatever the distance and the nature of the transfer involved and whether intra-day liquidity should be made available to banks in countries not part of the euro system who are none the less European Community members.

There is already a system for settling ecu transactions around the European Community. The Ecu Banking Association operates this system. At the end of each banking day it makes the necessary transfers between the member-state banks on a net basis through accounts at the Bank for International Settlement. This was to have been the ecu system and could have been developed into a system for the ecu as a single currency. Now that the Community has decided to substitute a different system based on a different currency the Ecu Banking Association faces the prospect of having a system for ecu settlement with no ecu to settle. As a result it has decided to switch its settlement system over to handling the euro. Instead of settling transactions between member-state banks across accounts at the Bank for International Settlement, they will seek to settle these accounts through the European system of central banks. They are therefore proposing a rival euro settlement system to the Target system being established *de novo* as part of the single-currency plans.

There is no objection in principle to having two rival systems of euro settlement. Some will say it will reduce the liquidity in either of the settlement systems, which could make it a little less smooth; others will say that it might mean extra costs. There is the offsetting possibility that having competitive settlement systems will keep them both up to the mark and limit the scope for either of them to try to charge a monopoly rent.

It is difficult to believe that the new euro Target settlement system will be cheaper than the systems it is replacing. A great deal of money will be spent on new computerized systems. Massive sums are already being spent on consultancy and planning. All this capital will need remunerating and repaying one way or another. The modest savings to international businesses because there will be no foreign-exchange transaction costs will in whole or part be offset by the additional costs needed for cash settlement and credit and paper settlement of transactions using the new automated settlement systems.

Large companies that have French and German as well as British and other international business will, of course, save the foreign-exchange transaction costs between the pound, the franc and the Deutschmark if all three countries join the Euro. They will not save foreign-exchange transaction costs into the yen or the dollar, nor will they save all money transmission and settlement costs.

For listed companies there will be some difficult transitional arrangements. Their share capital will need redenominating in euros instead of sterling. The Stock Exchange will have to change its listing rules, which currently include requirements in sterling. Listed companies may well decide to redenominate their shares in euros from the beginning of Stage 3. During the transitional period they will need to offer dividends in sterling as well as in euros. It is likely that each listed company will have to notify its shareholders of the changeover, seek their approval for changes in the share capital structure when it is redenominated and then circulate them again over their preferences for receiving dividends in sterling or in euros. Circulating shareholders for a public limited company is an expensive operation. The necessary steps may well entail several mailings.

Corporate accountants and lawyers are worried that the switch to the euro could also trigger tax liabilities. Under the current Commission proposals, when those currencies entering the scheme are irrevocably locked at the end of 1998, the Commission proposes that companies should have to present balance sheets denominated in euros and crystallize all the profits or losses on currencies at that point.

British companies have two important worries about this proposal. The first is that so doing could crystallize a tax liability, although the underlying changes in foreign exchange have not yet been realized. It is important that the tax authorities throughout the European Community should agree that the transition from national currencies to the euro should make no difference to the tax liability of the company concerned.

The second worry is that this proposal of the Commission will require companies to change their normal accounting procedures. It is not always good accounting procedure in Britain to crystallize all foreign-exchange losses or gains before the underlying contracts have been completed. It is one of many examples of how the Commission would use the existence of the single-currency scheme to change British and international accountancy arrangements without necessarily thinking through the business consequences.

No one has yet produced a reliable costing of the amount of investment involved. Preliminary suggestions point to £1,000m to change the banking system over to parallel running and then the introduction of the euro. This is likely to prove an underestimate. In the case of retailers, an independent European assessment has come up with the figure of £3,500m to switch over British shops. When account is taken of all the other changes needed in public limited companies and small businesses, the changing of all cash-handling and accounting systems, it is difficult to see how the final bill could be less than £10,000m. It is rather like imposing a 4 p surcharge on income tax on the country as a whole, as little of this investment will be remunerated. As one of the rules of the introduction is that prices should not go up as a result of the introduction of the new currency, the theorists of the scheme are proposing a £10,000m tax on British business with no means of direct benefit.

In practice, of course, it is likely that prices would go up as a result of the transitional period. Proponents of the single-currency scheme claim that the reward will come to business in the form of lower interest rates and in the form of saved foreign-exchange commissions. As we have seen, most businesses will have no savings on foreign exchange at all because they do not deal in foreign exchange at the moment. Those who do may well face increases in money transmission costs. We have also seen that lower interest rates are unlikely. The long-term real rate of interest has been higher in France and Germany than in Britain in the period 1980 to 1995, and it is difficult to see why this should change as a result of joining the euro bloc.

A £10,000m investment would normally require £2,500m a year of additional revenues to justify it. This would mean a 0.3 per cent increase in prices or raising our inflation rate by around 12 per cent. Proponents of the scheme have to explain why they think this would not happen. They should go back and look at what happened during the period of decimalization, when a much simpler and more modest change none the less triggered higher prices.

14

Transition – the proposals

The treaty is most detailed on how member states should move from having fifteen separate national currencies to one single currency. The second stage of the transition began on 1 January 1994. By that date every member state had to remove capital restrictions, permitting the free movement of monies between member states and with the outside world. They also had to put forward budgetary and economic plans to achieve low inflation and sound public finances. They were particularly requested to avoid excessive government deficits and are required to commence a process leading to the independence of each national central bank.

The European Monetary Institute (EMI) has been set up, replacing the old committee of governors of central banks. The council of the European Monetary Institute consists of a president and the governors of the national central banks. The EMI enjoys a series of powers and tasks. It has to strengthen cooperation between the national central banks, strengthen the coordination of the monetary policies of the member states with the aim of ensuring price stability, monitor the functioning of the European monetary system, hold consultations falling within the competence of the national central banks and affecting the stability of financial institutions and markets, take over the tasks of the European Monetary Cooperation Fund and facilitate the use of the ecu, overseeing its development and the smooth functioning of the ecu clearing system.

For the preparation of the third stage, the EMI shall:

prepare the instruments and procedures necessary for carrying out a single monetary policy in the third stage;

promote the harmonization, where necessary, of the rules and practices governing the collection, compilation and distribution of statistics in the areas within its field of competence;

prepare the rules for operations to be undertaken by the national central banks within the framework of the ESCB;

promote the efficiency of across-border payments;

supervise the technical preparation of ecu banknotes.

The European Monetary Institute acting on a two-thirds majority of its council members has the power to propose opinions or recommendations on monetary and exchange-rate policy introduced in each member state.

Throughout Article 109 it is made quite clear that the single currency will be the ecu. Article 109g tells us that the currency composition of the ecu basket will not be changed and goes on to state that from the start of the third stage of monetary union the value of the ecu should be irrevocably fixed. The third stage was originally to start before 1996. This was now been overtaken by events, so Article 109j4 applies. This Article says:

If by the end of 1997 the date for the beginning of the third stage has not been set, the third stage shall start on 1 January 1999. Before 1 July 1998, the Council, meeting in the composition of heads of state or of government, after a repetition of the procedure provided for in paragraphs 1 and 2, with the exception of the second indent of paragraph 2, taking into account the reports referred to in paragraph 1 and the opinion of the European Parliament, shall, acting by a qualified majority and on the basis of the recommendations of the Council referred to in paragraph 2, conform [sic] which member states fulfil the necessary conditions for the adoption of a single currency.

The reports referred to require an assessment of the degree of convergence achieved by each of the member states and an assessment of the member state's national legislation, especially relating to its central bank. The treaty accepts that on this delayed timetable it is quite likely that some states will not meet the requirements. They become member states with a derogation from joining until they have met the convergence requirements.

Immediately after the third-stage decision has been taken the European Central Bank is formally established. The EMI is liquidated. Member states joining the single currency decide unanimously the conversion rates 'at which their currencies shall be irrevocably fixed and at which irrevocably fixed rate the ecu shall be substituted for these currencies, and the ecu will become a currency in its own right. This measure shall by itself not modify the external value of the ecu. The council shall, acting according to the same procedure, also take the other measures necessary for the rapid introduction of the ecu as a single currency of those member states.'

The final part of Article 109m states,

Until the beginning of the third stage, each member state shall treat its exchange-rate policy as a matter of common interest. In so doing, member states shall take account of the experience required in cooperation within the framework of the European monetary system (EMS) and in developing the ecu, and shall respect existing powers in this field. From the beginning of the third stage and for as long as a member state has a derogation, paragraph 1 shall apply for analogy to the exchange-rate policy of that member state.

The idea behind the treaty is crystal clear from these explicit words in Article 109. Member states were to keep their currencies in close alignment one with another through the ERM. At the time the treaty was written the narrow bands of the ERM permitted only a 2¼ per cent fluctuation either way for a central rate for each currency. The treaty felt that if member states could maintain such stability between their exchange rates for a period of two years, it demonstrated that their economies were coming together. It meant that they could proceed from there to removing any fluctuation at all between the currencies.

The treaty is also clear that the currency which will replace the member states' currencies is the ecu. The ecu is a basket of European currencies. The composition of the basket is based on the relative size and strength of the economies underlying the national currencies. It has therefore been weaker than the strongest currencies in Europe and stronger than the weakest currencies, being a weighted average. Its daily rate has been calculated for many years. It has been possible for some time to hold ecu bank accounts, to send out invoices in ecus and to calculate grants, subsidies, business turnover and costs in ecus. There have been a few ecu coins issued, but in the main it has been a banker's currency used by big business and government to borrow money and to lend money and sometimes to keep account. There has not been a universal note or coin issue to make it like the pound or the Deutschmark.

Again, the treaty envisaged a smooth transition. The authors of the treaty decided that in the run-up to monetary union the practice of using ecu bank accounts, sending out ecu invoices, collecting ecu receivables and lending and borrowing in ecus would develop apace. Once in Stage 3 the member states' currencies had been fixed at a permanent and constant exchange rate into ecus, so the ecu market had effectively been transformed. Then the laborious process could begin of issuing enough ecu banknotes and coins to take over from national currencies throughout the European single-currency area. At this point the ecu would become a true currency, replacing the Deutschmark or the franc or the pound.

The treaty is so explicit about this system that no one reading it can be in any doubt that the single currency is to be the ecu. Nor can anyone be in any doubt that the idea of convergence was primarily based on the convergence of currencies. That was why so much effort was put in to building and maintaining the ERM and why its dissolution in 1992 was such a blow to those who were hoping to build a European federal state.

In the aftermath of the destruction of the narrow-band ERM, a great deal of reinterpretation has been undertaken. Apologists for the single currency now say that the question of what the new currency should be called was always left open in the treaty and could be settled at a later date. At subsequent meetings, after a great deal of wrangling about whether the single currency should be called the florin or the schilling or the Euro mark/Euro franc/ Euro pound or the ecu or something else, the member states finally agreed to call it the euro.

Some have seen in the change of name the advantage that it now appears that the failure of the member states' currencies to stay in line roughly with the ecu no longer matters to the success of monetary union. Although the main emphasis of the treaty is on bringing currencies into alignment one with another, in recent months all attention has shifted to the budget-deficit requirements as if they were the only or main requirements of the treaty.

European officials now accept that several currencies in the ERM need bands as wide as 15 per cent fluctuation either way in order to maintain their precarious 'stability' within the system. Allowing currencies 30 per cent tolerance takes care of all but the wildest fluctuations and the most extreme divergences of policy. It is tantamount to having no exchange-rate system at all. Yet so low are the ambitions now with respect to currency stability, that maintaining plus or minus 15 per cent is thought to be perfectly adequate.

Some countries are no longer in the ERM. Many accept that Britain, although not a member of the ERM, could somehow nevertheless be given permission to abolish the pound and join the single currency. It is assumed that people would make out graphs of our currency fluctuation and, if they were well disposed to our joining the system, would conclude that our currency fluctuation was not outside the terms of the treaty even though we had not been ERM members for the relevant period. Again, there would be no legal basis whatsoever for this judgement, given the very clear words of the treaty.

The handling of the transitional period has been dogged by misjudgement and bad luck throughout. Having decided to abandon all pretence at bringing exchange rates into line by narrowing the fluctuation bands, the member states and officials have turned instead to concentrating on the convergence of budget deficits. There is every reason to do this as all will be borrowing in the same currency at an identical or very similar interest rate once the single currency has been established. Even this has proved to be far more vexatious than the framers of the treaty imagined. They expected the background to be reasonable growth and prosperity in the European economies as a whole. They imagined that holding every country to a maximum level of borrowing of 3 per cent of its national output would be comparatively easy. Certainly the Germans never anticipated that they themselves would find it difficult if not impossible to get their budget deficit down to the required level. In 1992 the single market of the European Community formally reached maturity. Many European politicians believed the hype surrounding this development. It was confidently said at the time that the creation of the single market itself would add 3 per cent to European national income. This would have represented a colossal increase in national income and wealth and would indeed have been well worth while. Unfortunately, the formal advent of the completed single market saw a downturn in the growth rate across the European continent which has still not recovered. I do not blame the single market for the drop in the growth rate – but I do not think that if there had been no single market the European economies would have fallen 3 per cent further.

The whole single-market scheme was ill-conceived and over-egged. Removing restrictions and barriers to trade between the companies and peoples of Western Europe will indeed increase the growth rate and prosperity level. Many European politicians, however, saw the single-market policy as an opportunity to increase the powers of European central government by a huge raft of new legislation and regulation. Some of this, far from increasing prosperity and removing barriers, created new obstacles and new barriers and was damaging to prosperity. A large number of the directives took the form of prescribing in law and regulation how individual products could or could not be made. Legislators said this would help the single market because it meant that every factory and company in Western Europe would operate to the same standard, permitting customers a wider choice of which producer supplied them the goods. It also meant that the ability to innovate and keep up with the newest technology was stifled: it became illegal to develop certain types of new technology or to change or improve products in certain ways. Far from promoting faster growth and prosperity in some sectors this became a modest deterrent to it. Similarly, in financial services measures which were presented as necessary to allow a customer in Germany to buy a British insurance policy or vice versa rapidly became ways of increasing the general regulatory burden on all insurance companies across Western Europe. Far from lowering costs and sharpening competition they became methods of raising costs and creating new barriers to new competition.

As a result, the completion of the legal framework of the single market was probably at best neutral for its impact on European growth. The reason the run-up to the single-currency scheme was dogged by low growth and rising budget deficits lay in the ERM and the monetary policies it required. Although the mechanism did not work and had to be fundamentally revised, permitting much wider bands, even the wider bands acted as a considerable restraint on the monetary policies of various member states.

It will be recorded as one of those ironies of history that a system designed to create a virtuous cycle of reasonable growth, low inflation and expanding prosperity succeeded in creating a vicious cycle in every respect save the reduction of inflation. The Germans got their way. Controlling inflation became not only the main but effectively the only economic goal being pursued.

Can the transition to a single currency work? There is no doubt that the transitional scheme envisaged in the treaty is a dead letter. There is no way now that member states can gradually reduce their exchange-rate fluctuations so that replacing their domestic currencies by the ecu is a mere formality. That idea is as dead as a dodo. So much so that the architects of the idea have now turned round and claimed that was never what they intended in the first place, despite the words of the treaty reminding us that that was the scheme. Today the transitional approach is rather different. Member states by the end of 1997 have to report their progress. They will have to explain what they have done in controlling their budget deficits, getting down their inflation rates, bringing their long-term interest rates into line with those of their partners and, presumably, what has happened to their exchange rate. All those who have survived within the plus or minus 15 per cent ERM will deem themselves to have qualified regardless. The others could table their exchange-rate progress and demonstrate that they too had been close to being within plus or minus 15 per cent.

The member states themselves then decide which countries if any have qualified under the criteria. There is some latitude in the budget-deficit and the stock-of-debt criteria. If member states also wish to interpret the currency variable flexibly they will doubtless do so. Looking at the figures it seems quite likely that the member states themselves might decide that France, Germany, Luxembourg, Austria and The Netherlands have qualified. Although Belgium clearly cannot qualify, given its stock of public debt, there could well be some reinterpretation or representation of the Belgian figures, as many people will see a single currency without Belgium as an absurdity. There needs to be a minimum of four countries going ahead.

The big question for us is whether the United Kingdom will want to apply or not. The UK would be able to qualify, assuming that she had legislated to make the Bank of England independent and assuming the member states decided not to worry about ERM membership. The United Kingdom will be one of the few that does qualify on the debt requirement, and will have one of the lower budget deficits of the potential participants. The UK's inflation rate might be close enough and interest rates have come down. If the United Kingdom decides to go ahead it is quite likely the Republic of Ireland as well will be more enthusiastic. It might even influence the attitude of the Danish government, the only other country with a right not to join and a public hostile to it.

In the situation where only a small core group of countries

including France, Germany and Benelux are able and willing to go ahead, the United Kingdom could play a most important role. The southern countries might be very worried to see the core countries moving quickly to economic and monetary union, which would inevitably lead to political union. They would see themselves in a second division or even excluded from the game altogether. French and German diplomacy in such a circumstance would be geared to trying to reassure them that it is only a matter of time, that they would be able to join eventually. However, it is difficult to see how a country like Italy could ever join, given its high level of public debt, or how within a reasonable time-scale Spain, Greece and Portugal could be brought into line with the core economies. British diplomacy could play on these fears of exclusion, forming an alliance of the majority of countries who either will not be able to join or who do not wish to join in the first phase. Such an alliance could insist on much stricter interpretation of the criteria to make it as difficult as possible for any country to join the scheme.

In such a position the French and Germans would be faced with a dilemma. The British-led coalition would be pointing out that France had not met the ERM criteria as properly interpreted, that France, Germany and the Benelux countries were not meeting the debt criteria and that therefore they too were unable to move ahead. If France and Germany wished to sweep aside this disagreement they would be unable to do so easily. They could not amend the treaty as any treaty amendment would require unanimity. Britain on her own can stop any watering down the convergence criteria. If they wished to go ahead with a favourable interpretation of the treaty they will need at least a qualified majority of the votes of the member states in order to reinterpret the treaty with some semblance of legality.

Careful diplomacy by Britain could be decisive. A Britain determined to prevent Europe from the folly of a single currency could mobilize the excluded and the worried, and insist upon an even stricter view of the requirements of the treaty than the German government is proposing. Such a diplomatic effort would produce some interesting alliances. Many Germans would agree with the view that the criteria have to be firmly adhered to. The German Central Bank would undoubtedly agree. Many in the excluded south of the European Community would be pleased at the thought that the whole process could be slowed down.

Conversely, the United Kingdom could use its diplomatic strength to ensure that the single-currency scheme does go ahead. If the United Kingdom wanted to join and allied itself with those states wishing to take a more flexible view of the treaty, that could prove decisive. The United Kingdom could be important in reassuring the south that they would be let in through a flexible interpretation of the criteria at a later date. Without British leadership it is unlikely that the countries of the south on their own would try to derail the single-currency programme. Traditional southern diplomacy is more likely to seek a watering-down of the requirements for themselves or compensatory measures for their own economies in the mistaken belief that this might speed up their own convergence.

A United Kingdom committed to the single-currency project would be able to join and could be instrumental in calming down other worries. Britain's position is therefore pivotal. Britain will not have decisive influence if she refuses to make up her mind.

There are three possible positions that the United Kingdom can adopt. The first is wholesale opposition, with a view to stopping the whole project. That is what I favour. The second would be wholehearted acceptance of the project, with Britain using her diplomatic weight to help bring it to fruition. The third would be for Britain to say that a single currency is desirable in principle but that a new scheme is needed, given the chaos that we have seen so far.

The United Kingdom could say, for example, that we need to go back to the original idea. Countries wishing to join the single currency should keep their currencies in line with one another in progressively tightening bands. Only when they have demonstrated their ability to do that, should they then go on to replacing their national currencies. Alternatively, the United Kingdom could say that the architecture of the treaty is wrong and that what is needed is a new set of criteria taking more account of growth and the real economy. If you really wish to live together as one country it would make more sense if income per head, output per head, productivity and employment levels were comparable between the different parts of the currency union. If they are not, there will need to be very large transfer payments from one part to another and there will be growing disappointment in the areas which start from behind when they find it is even more difficult to catch up within a single-currency area than it was when they had their own exchange rate. It would be possible to devise a series of proper real convergence measures.

It would be a good idea to set a maximum level of unemployment. If the United Kingdom proposed a maximum unemployment level and said that no member state was allowed to deviate by more than two percentage points from a central rate of say 7½ per cent, it would greatly ease the pains and troubles of transition within a currency union. Similarly, Britain could propose that participating parts of the union should commence with a real level of national income per head that does not deviate by more than 10 per cent from the average. A similar figure could be imposed upon an agreed measure of productivity. Ideally this would be in addition to bringing currencies into line with one another.

Those who wish to see a single currency would immediately object that these criteria would be far too stringent, meaning interminable delay, even the effective end of the idea of a single currency. That could be the case. It shows how foolish it would be to go ahead if anything less is achieved. A currency union with wildly different unemployment rates between the different parts of the union would impose intolerable strains. Without real economic convergence the union would be in danger of creating a series of depressed areas, towns and cities which would find it even more difficult to get out of depression.

It is a great sadness that Western European politicians are now so out of touch with their electors that they believe monetary union is what is wanted rather than lower unemployment. Yet the main concern of the people themselves is the very high levels of unemployment they are facing. One in 4 of all Spaniards of working age are without jobs, 1 in 8 of all French people, 1 in 8 of all Italians and 1 in 8 of all Germans. This is the true crisis facing Western Europe and it is the direct result of the scheme of monetary union.

Instead of more laws and regulations, and more central control, the markets need more breathing space to create jobs. The European Community is lobbied by and responds to big businesses to a much greater extent than small. It is to the small businesses that we need to look for recovery from the unemployment crisis. The European Union is looking in the opposite direction.

It is difficult to predict what will happen now, as so much rests upon the attitude of the United Kingdom. It seems to be a fact of life that the French President and the German Chancellor are determined to press ahead with the currency union whatever the cost. It also seems very likely that the German Chancellor will make ever more compromises over the scheme and over the pursuit of the low-inflation objective in the interests of bringing it off. While some relaxation will be welcome from the point of view of growth, we will still end up with a set of European policies that are more damaging to the member states' economies than if they had gone it alone and sorted out their own economic difficulties in their own way. If Britain weighs in heavily against the scheme, it would be possible to stop it in its tracks. If Britain weighs in enthusiastically in favour, it will undoubtedly carry. That is why the debate in Britain is so central to the whole question. People across Europe are watching Britain with a mixture of fascination and, in the case of the federalists, despair. The battleground of Europe was once the Danish referendum. It then moved on to the French referendum. Now it is the British political and parliamentary process.

I do not believe either major political party in Britain could put through the abolition of the pound without doing grave damage to itself. Both the Conservative and the Labour parties contain a

significant number of Members of Parliament who could not tolerate the abolition of the pound. If either party in power wished to
press ahead it would be dependent upon a combination of their
own payroll votes and the votes of the Euro-enthusiasts on both
sides of the House. It would not be easy to reunite the political
party that carried out such an act of divisive folly. The Maastricht
debate showed how explosive these matters are. Despite the heavy
whipping, fifty Conservative MPs at one stage or another of the
proceedings rebelled and the government only carried its business
because opposition parties were prepared to back it on many crucial
votes. The single-currency debate would be far more intense and
far worse, and there would be many more rebels on both sides.

Europe awaits. In the meantime, Germany is allowing her interest rates to fall as the Chancellor attempts to relieve some of the
pressures on the French economy. They seem to have at last
realized that it would be easier to push forward with monetary
union if monetary policy were easier, inflation rates a little higher
and growth a bit better. Lukewarm attempts are made to improve
the continental economies while the people of Western Europe
grow more desperate in the face of high unemployment. The
transition is being handled extremely badly. Many are now disillu-
sioned with the whole process, and fed up with the damage it has
already done.

15

Can any country qualify for the single currency?

The first European Monetary Institute report is an excellent account of the difficulties countries experienced up to September 1996 in preparing for the single currency. It made clear the basis on which it would interpret the requirements:

first, the individual criteria are interpreted and applied in a strict manner. The rationale behind this principle . . . is that the main purpose of the criteria is to ensure that only those member states which have economic conditions that are conducive to the maintenance of price stability and the viability of the European currency area should participate in it. Second, the convergence criteria constituted a coherent and integrated package and they must all be satisfied; the treaty lists the criteria on an equal footing and does not suggest hierarchy. Third, the convergence criteria have to be met on the basis of the current data. Fourth, the application of the convergence criteria should be consistent, transparent and simple.

In the twelve-month period to the end of September 1996 the three best performing countries for price stability were Finland, The Netherlands and Germany. Finnish prices increased by 0.9 per cent, Dutch prices by 1.2 per cent and German by 1.3 per cent. This means that all other countries have to achieve a rate no higher than 2.6 per cent, 1½ percentage points above the average of the best three. On this basis Greece at 8.4 per cent, Italy at 4.7 per cent, Spain at 3.8 per cent, and Portugal and the United Kingdom at 3 per cent are all above the reference level and unable to qualify.

In the year to September 1996 ten-year government bond yields in the three best performing countries for inflation ranged between

Table 8 Economic indicators and the Maastrict Treaty convergence criteria *(excluding the exchange-rate criterion)*

		Inflation (%)	Long-term interest rate (%)	General gov. lending (+) or borrowing(−) % of GDP	General gov. gross debt, % of GDP
Belgium	1995	1.4	7.5	−4.1	133.7
	1996	1.6	6.7	−3.3	130.6
Denmark	1995	2.3	8.3	−1.6	71.9
	1996	2.2	7.4	−1.4	70.2
Germany	1995	1.5	6.9	−3.5	58.1
	1996	1.3	6.3	−4.0	60.8
Greece	1995	9.0	17.4	−9.1	111.8
	1996	8.4	15.1	−7.9	110.6
Spain	1995	4.7	11.3	−6.6	65.7
	1996	3.8	9.5	−4.4	67.8
France	1995	1.7	7.5	−4.8	52.8
	1996	2.1	6.6	−4.0	56.4
Ireland	1995	2.4	8.3	−2.0	81.6
	1996	2.1	7.5	−1.6	74.7
Italy	1995	5.4	12.2	−7.1	124.9
	1996	4.7	10.3	−6.6	123.4
Luxembourg	1995	1.9	7.6	1.5	6.0
	1996	1.3	7.0	0.9	7.8
Netherlands	1995	1.1	6.9	−4.0	79.7
	1996	1.2	6.3	−2.6	78.7
Austria	1995	2.0	7.1	−5.9	69.0
	1996	1.7	6.5	−4.3	71.1
Portugal	1995	3.8	11.5	−5.1	71.7
	1996	3.0	9.4	−4.0	71.7
Finland	1995	1.0	8.8	−5.2	59.2
	1996	0.9	7.4	−3.3	61.3
Sweden	1995	2.9	10.2	−8.1	78.7
	1996	1.6	8.5	−3.9	78.1
UK	1995	3.1	8.3	−5.8	54.1
	1996	3.0	8.0	−4.6	56.3

Table 9   Interim indices of consumer price inflation (*annual percentage rates*)

	1995	Oct. 95 –Sep. 96	Q4 95	Q1 96	Q2 96	Q3 96
Belgium	1.4	1.6	1.2	1.7	1.7	2.0
Denmark	2.3	3.3	2.2	2.0	2.2	2.5
Germany	1.5	1.3	1.4	1.4	1.3	1.3
Greece	9.0	8.4	8.0	8.4	8.8	8.3
Spain	4.7	3.8	4.3	3.6	3.6	3.7
France	1.7	2.1	2.0	2.2	2.5	1.9
Ireland	2.4	2.1	2.3	2.1	1.9	2.2
Italy	5.4	4.7	5.8	5.1	4.3	3.5
Luxembourg	1.9	1.3	1.4	1.1	1.5	1.4
Netherlands	1.1	1.2	0.7	1.3	1.4	1.5
Austria	2.0	1.7	1.6	1.5	1.7	2.1
Portugal	3.8	3.0	3.5	2.3	3.0	3.4
Finland	1.0	0.9	0.3	0.9	1.3	1.1
Sweden	2.9	1.6	2.9	1.4	1.1	0.8
UK	3.1	3.0	3.3	3.1	2.9	2.9
Memo items: EU-15	3.0	2.7	2.9	2.7	2.6	2.4

6.3 per cent and 7.4 per cent. The reference ceiling is therefore 8.7 per cent, 1½ percentage points over the average of the three best performing countries. This means that Greece with long-term interest rates of 15.1 per cent, Italy at 10.3 per cent, Spain at 9.5 per cent and Portugal at 9.4 per cent do not meet the requirements on those data. Given that Greece, Spain, Italy and Portugal fail to meet the government debt requirements as well as the inflation and the long-term interest-rate requirements, it is looking extremely unlikely that they are going to get anywhere near meeting the

	Apr. 96	May 96	June 96	July 96	Aug. 96	Sept. 96
Belgium	1.9	1.7	1.7	1.9	2.0	2.1
Denmark	2.2	2.1	2.2	2.6	2.5	2.5
Germany	1.5	1.4	1.1	1.4	1.2	1.3
Greece	9.0	8.9	8.5	8.4	8.3	8.1
Spain	3.4	3.7	3.5	3.7	3.7	3.6
France	2.6	2.6	2.4	2.4	1.7	1.6
Ireland	1.9	1.9	1.9	2.2	2.2	2.2
Italy	4.5	4.5	4.0	3.7	3.5	3.5
Luxembourg	1.6	1.5	1.4	1.4	1.5	1.5
Netherlands	1.6	1.5	1.1	1.7	1.3	1.4
Austria	2.0	1.5	1.7	2.1	2.2	2.2
Portugal	2.6	3.1	3.3	3.5	3.5	3.2
Finland	1.2	1.5	1.2	1.1	1.1	1.2
Sweden	1.3	1.2	1.0	1.0	0.8	0.6
UK	3.0	2.8	2.9	2.9	2.8	2.9
Memo items: EU-15	2.7	2.6	2.5	2.5	2.3	2.4

requirements to join in 1999. Their economies are simply too different and diverge far too far from the French and German economies to make it feasible.

The most problematic requirements for all member states are those concerning the government deficit, government borrowing and the government budgetary position. Governments are not meant to borrow more than 3 per cent of their national income in any given year. The most recent figures available show only Denmark at 1.4 per cent, Ireland at 1.6 per cent, Luxembourg at

Table 10   General government gross debt *(as a percentage of GDP)*

General government net lending (+) / net borrowing (−)

	1991	1992	1993	1994	1995	1996
Belgium	−6.5	−7.2	−7.5	−5.1	−4.1	−3.3
Denmark	−2.1	−2.9	−3.9	−3.5	−1.6	−1.4
Germany	−3.3	−2.8	−3.5	−2.4	−3.5	−4.0
Greece	−11.5	−12.3	−14.2	−12.1	−9.1	−7.9
Spain	−4.9	−3.6	−6.8	−6.3	−16.6	−4.4
France	−2.2	−3.8	−5.6	−5.6	−4.8	−4.0
Ireland	−2.3	−2.5	−2.4	−1.7	−2.0	−1.6
Italy	−10.2	−9.5	−9.6	−9.0	−7.1	−6.6
Luxembourg	1.9	0.8	1.7	2.6	1.5	0.9
Netherlands	−2.9	−3.9	−3.2	−3.4	−4.0	−2.6
Austria	−2.6	−1.9	−4.2	−4.4	−5.9	−4.3
Portugal	−6.7	−3.6	−6.9	−5.8	−5.1	−4.0
Finland	−1.5	−5.9	−8.0	−6.2	−5.2	−3.3
Sweden	−1.1	−7.8	−12.3	−10.8	−8.1	−3.9
UK	−2.6	−6.3	−7.8	−6.8	−5.8	−4.6
EU-15	−4.3	−5.1	−6.2	−5.4	−5.0	−4.4

0.9 per cent and The Netherlands at 2.6 per cent meeting this requirement. All the others exceeded it, some by a large margin. Greece is borrowing 7.9 per cent of national income, Italy 6.6 per cent, the United Kingdom 4.6 per cent, Austria 4.3 per cent and Spain 4.4 per cent. Countries are also meant to keep their general government gross debt to below 60 per cent of their national income. Only Luxembourg, France and the United Kingdom have succeeded in doing that. Some countries are massively over the requirement. The list is headed by Belgium which has borrowed 130.6 per cent of its national income. Italy is almost as bad at 123.4 per cent, and Greece at 110.6 per cent. Sweden and The

General government gross debt

	1991	1992	1993	1994	1995	1996
Belgium	129.4	130.6	137.0	135.0	133.7	130.6
Denmark	64.6	68.7	80.1	76.0	71.9	70.2
Germany	41.5	44.1	48.2	50.4	58.1	60.8
Greece	92.3	99.2	111.8	110.4	111.8	110.6
Spain	45.8	48.4	60.5	63.1	65.7	67.8
France	35.8	39.6	45.6	48.4	52.8	56.4
Ireland	95.0	92.0	94.5	87.9	81.6	74.7
Italy	101.4	108.5	119.3	125.5	124.9	123.4
Luxembourg	4.2	5.2	6.2	5.7	6.0	7.8
Netherlands	78.8	79.6	80.8	77.4	79.7	78.7
Austria	58.7	58.3	62.8	65.1	69.0	71.7
Portugal	71.1	63.3	68.2	69.6	71.7	71.1
Finland	23.0	41.5	57.3	59.5	59.2	61.3
Sweden	53.0	67.1	76.0	79.3	78.7	78.1
UK	35.7	41.9	48.5	50.4	54.1	56.3
EU-15	56.1	60.4	66.1	68.1	71.3	73.5

Netherlands both exceed 78 per cent, Austria, Portugal, Ireland and Denmark also exceed 70 per cent. Although Germany's level is only 60.8 per cent, it has been rising sharply in recent years, as has Finland's at 61.3 per cent.

Even the EMI, a keen advocate of monetary union, is perturbed by the lack of progress on the debt front. It states 'progress in fiscal consolidation has generally been too slow. Deficits continue to be a cause of great concern and, in general, faster correction of fiscal imbalances is warranted.' In code the EMI is saying clearly that taxes have to go up or spending has to be reduced so that running deficits are cut and the amount of debt outstanding relative to

GNP is also reduced. In many cases this would mean not merely getting below the 3 per cent deficit requirement, but moving the country into surplus so that the total stock of debt can be reduced. The EMI concludes: 'most countries have not yet achieved a situation which, in a broader view, might be judged as sustainable in the medium term. This is clearly shown by worrisome debt developments.'

The Community should be honest. It should accept that most member states are not going to get their debt down to 60 per cent of GNP or anything like it. No amount of weaving, ducking or fudging can disguise the fact that the stock of debt requirement is too stiff for the member states to meet. Either they have to abandon the scheme or they need to amend the treaty, taking out the 60 per cent figure and putting in a figure of around 80–100 per cent.

It has not been much easier keeping the currencies together. EMI reports that a number of currencies remain stable including the Belgium/Luxembourg franc, the DM, the Dutch guilder, the Austrian Schilling. The krona, the French franc and the Irish punt have drifted away from their central parities, although by September 1996 they had returned to close to their central rates. In March 1995 the Spanish peseta was devalued by 7 per cent. The Portuguese escudo followed with a devaluation of 3½ per cent. The EMI concludes that, outside the ERM, 'the Finnish markka remained broadly stable throughout the period under consideration – as did, to a lesser extent, the Greek drachma. In contrast, the Italian lira and the pound sterling underwent periods of turbulence, followed by a complete or partial recovery. The Swedish krona also experienced a period of turbulence but appreciated significantly over the two-year reference period considered.' This is a polite way of saying that over half the currencies of the European Community deviated dramatically from their central rates for a greater or shorter time, illustrating that the Community was a long way away from the convergence of currencies envisaged in the original single-currency scheme.

Central banks also have to be sufficiently independent for the member state to qualify for single-currency membership. Article 107 of the treaty and Article 14.2 of the statute contain a prohibition of external influence on the European Central Bank, national central banks and members of their decision-making bodies, and provides for the security of tenure of the members. The EMI has concluded that in order to fulfil this part of the treaty the rights of third parties like government and parliament to give instructions to national central banks to approve, suspend, annul or defer their decisions, to censure a national central bank's decision on legal grounds, to participate in the decision-making bodies of such a bank or to be consulted beforehand on its decisions are incompatible with the treaty and/or the statute.

National central bank governors should have a minimum term of office of five years. The governor should not be dismissed for reasons other than those mentioned in Article 14.2 of the statute, confining removal from office to no longer fulfilling the conditions for the performance of the duties or being guilty of serious misconduct. Other board members should have the same security of tenure as governors and no conflicts of interest should arise. Functional independence requires the statutory objectives of a central bank to be in line with the European system of a central bank's objectives as laid down in Article 2 of its statute.

In order to qualify, Belgium is proposing a new law to entrench central bank independence; Luxembourg's law needs substantial amendment; Finland is planning legislation. Denmark has opted out of participation in monetary union so it does not have to adapt. Even the German central bank needs to entrench a guaranteed minimum five-year term of office for members of the bank's decision-making bodies and needs to amend the statute to reflect unambiguously the primacy of maintaining price stability as the objective. So far no changes to the bank's statute have been planned or notified to the EMI.

The Greek central bank, too, needs an amended statute. Apparently the bank's monetary decisions are subordinated to the government's macro-economic objectives, but this will have to alter.

Table 11   Summary of changes in real effective exchange rates of
EU-15 currencies up to September 1996 *(monthly data in percentages)*

a) since 1987

	CPI	ULC	XPI	PPI
Belgium	0.6	9.4	−1.4	1.4
Denmark	1.0	11.0	−1.0	6.1
Germany	4.8	19.9	−3.9	4.3
Spain	4.7	2.4	−1.2	3.8
France	−1.5	−6.5	1.8	−0.5
Ireland	−6.6	−26.9	−6.0	−1.5
Netherlands	−1.8	−6.8	−2.6	3.1
Austria	2.4	−10.2	−20.3	−0.9
Portugal*	27.2	–	−4.6	–
Greece†	26.0	30.9	–	12.9
Italy	−10.4	−12.8	−12.8	−11.2
Finland	−13.1	−22.5	6.3	−8.9
Sweden	−1.0	−10.5	3.2	2.5
UK	−3.6	−8.9	3.1	3.7

CPI Deflated by consumer prices
ULC Deflated by unit labour costs
XPI Deflated by export prices
PPI Deflated by producer price indices
*ULC and PPI indicators are not presented because reliable series are not available
for Portugal
†XPI indicators are not presented because reliable series are not available for Greece

This table shows changes in currency rates adjusted for differences in prices and
costs of producing goods. This is an attempt to show how export prices become
dearer or cheaper depending on currency changes.

b) since April 1992

	CPI	ULC	XPI	PPI
Belgium	4.8	9.9	−6.8	3.8
Denmark	5.8	13.8	1.7	7.5
Germany	8.1	17.1	−1.0	4.1
Spain	−13.1	−20.8	−13.2	−10.1
France	4.1	−1.2	−1.4	3.1
Ireland	−1.5	−16.5	−3.0	0.9
Netherlands	5.9	1.3	1.8	4.8
Austria	5.8	−2.1	−11.9	−0.3
Portugal*	0.5	–	−2.4	–
Greece†	11.3	15.0	–	5.6
Italy	−15.8	−20.6	8.1	−12.8
Finland	−7.7	−12.6	7.5	−0.5
Sweden	−12.9	−21.9	−0.5	−2.7
UK	−15.0	−11.3	−2.9	−7.9

c) since October 1994

	CPI	ULC	XPI	PPI
Belgium	−0.1	1.3	−4.1	0.7
Denmark	2.2	6.3	−2.2	2.8
Germany	−0.3	3.6	1.3	−0.8
Spain	2.8	−1.2	0.8	4.9
France	0.4	−3.9	−7.1	−0.6
Ireland	1.6	−7.4	−1.0	1.9
Netherlands	−0.1	−2.0	−1.2	0.3
Austria	0.7	−2.9	−10.8	−4.5
Portugal*	3.1	–	−0.9	–
Greece†	8.2	16.1	–	5.1
Italy	6.6	4.7	19.5	7.2
Finland	−0.9	1.7	5.2	0.6
Sweden	7.3	8.3	11.5	11.2
UK	−1.5	0.5	−1.6	−0.2

Minimum five-year terms of office should be guaranteed for the governor and other members of the general council. Spain has to increase the term of office when electing members of the governing council of its bank, while in France there needs to be an extension of the independence to cover all areas related to the European Central Bank's activities. The Bank of Ireland has to make it clear that the governor attending the subcommittee of the House of Representatives has to respect the secrecy provisions of the treaty and the grounds for dismissal of the governor have to be brought into line with the treaty. The draft law for the Bank of Ireland has been published, but it does not yet go far enough to meet the treaty requirements. The Italian central bank needs a new statute to put the primacy of price stability as its main objective. The power of the minister of the treasury to fix interest rates on certain interest-bearing current-account deposits with the bank also needs to be changed.

Luxembourg law needs substantial amendment. Competence for monetary policy is currently vested in the government and needs to be transferred to the bank. The personal independence of the members of the council of the Institute Monétaire Luxembourgeois needs to be strengthened. Its members need security of tenure with a five-year minimum period of office. Holland is planning thorough-going reform in order to bring its central bank rules into line. Austria needs to change the right of the State Commissioner to examine the Banks acts, and to strengthen the independence and composition of its general council. Portugal needs to stop the minister of finance signing the bank's directions relating to some features of the reserves requirement's framework and the discount rate. Finland is planning legislation to bring its requirements into line with the treaty but the EMI concludes that it does not go far enough. The Swedish bank's constitution is in conflict, especially the obligation for the bank to consult the minister of finance on decisions of major importance.

If the United Kingdom is to join the single currency monetary policy would have to be transferred from the government to the

Bank. The Treasury would no longer retain power to issue directions to the Bank and the Bank's advisory role in the conduct of monetary policy would be changed to a decisive role as part of the European System of Central Banks. The appearance of the governor before committees of Parliament would need to be limited as he would need to maintain secrecy governing matters of common interest for the European System of Central Banks. The statutory objective of the Bank would have to be changed to reflect unambiguously the primacy of maintaining price stability.

The need to make fundamental changes to the conduct of monetary policy in the statutes of most central banks in the union shows what a fundamental change is under way. In the case of the United Kingdom it would be a reversal of the current position. Today the government is ultimately responsible for economic and monetary policy. The Bank of England operating under its statute has an important advisory role. This advisory role has recently been strengthened by the publication of the Minutes of the monthly meeting held between the Chancellor of the Exchequer and the Governor of the Bank of England to discuss the monetary position and to settle interest rates. Under a single-currency scheme there could be no such meeting. The Governor of the Bank of England acting alone in Britain on behalf of the interests of the European System of Central Banks would make decisions about monetary growth, inflation and interest rates. He would tell the government and the country of his decisions after they had been made and there would be no right or duty for the Chancellor, any elected parliamentarian or other government official to influence or affect these decisions.

While the Governor would still be allowed to come to the House of Commons to answer questions or to report to select committees, as he is currently required to do, the ground rules for the conduct of such meetings are plain. The Parliament must bring no power or influence to bear to get the Governor to change his mind about the future conduct of monetary policy. While the Parliament could go over the grounds and reasoning behind the changes made to date, they would not be able to make recommendations for the future or to seek through their method of questioning to propose an alternative course of action. The Chancellor would have surrendered all his power over monetary policy and interest rates to the Governor and to the European system. The Governor himself would have limited scope for manoeuvre. The statute would require him to follow as a matter of policy the pursuit of price stability. There could be no argument about tolerating a little more inflation in order to bring unemployment down or while transition to zero inflation was being made. The sole thought in the Governor's mind whenever he settled interest rates would have to be the pursuit of zero inflation. The Governor would also be the factotum or agent of the European system and in due course of the European Central Bank. There would be a common monetary policy for Europe as a whole determined around the table of the European Central Bank. Interest rates settled there would apply in all the countries which had joined the monetary union, regardless of the economic conditions in the separate countries.

Parliament might well be concerned when it realizes just how circumscribed its power to influence debate, question and discuss will become under such a system. German and Commission influence has been strong. There is a passion to pursue zero inflation at the expense of other economic objectives. There is a recognition that allowing political intervention makes this less likely. As a result they have designed a system which will conduct economic policy on auto-pilot, charting a course of zero inflation. Most existing central banks do not have the pursuit of price stability as their sole or prime aim. In practically every case they allow politicians to dismiss governors and members of the governing board in certain circumstances beyond those defined in the treaty. Most also allow elected ministers to influence, guide or decide monetary policy, because all these countries are lively democracies.

It is the intention of the European system to remove democratic accountability and influence from monetary policy, believing that a group of technicians around the Central Bank table will be able to do a much better job than the elected politicians. No one has thought to ask the question what will happen if they do not succeed. Of course, if as a result of a transition to an independent system we had zero inflation, 3 per cent growth, unemployment at 2 per cent or below and higher incomes, everybody would be satisfied even though they had lost democratic control over the process. But if the process delivers less than this, if unemployment stays high or rises, if inflation does not plummet to zero, if too many businesses go bust through lack of credit, if interest rates are too high, the electorates will want to make their views known. In this system, there will be no way of letting the pressure out. The valve in the pressure cooker will have been soldered over, and as the temperature rises, as people become more disenchanted with the economic and monetary policy being pursued, the pressure will build up.

At present, only Luxembourg could properly qualify for the single currency as designed in the Treaty of Maastricht. Only Luxembourg sails through all the tests. Luxembourg alone is well below the 60 per cent debt ceiling, is borrowing very little year by year, has low inflation, low interest rates and could make the necessary changes to its central bank arrangements. We have seen how five countries are so far beyond all the requirements they have no chance of joining on any sensible interpretation. Only France, the United Kingdom and Luxembourg are below the 60 per cent government-borrowing-to-national-income ceiling, and France is going to find it difficult if not impossible to meet the 3 per cent budget deficit requirement. Britain has not rejoined the ERM and cannot meet the currency requirement.

It is confidently expected that when the decision comes to be made in the first half of 1998 a more tolerant view will be taken of the requirements: possibly, if a country is still above 3 per cent borrowing as a proportion of national income but is moving down or has borrowed more than 60 per cent but the proportion is declining, then that would be sufficient. Such interpretations would not, however, be legal unless the treaty were properly amended to put the matter beyond doubt. All these things can be subject to litigation and big money rides on them.

The original requirements were put into the Treaty of Maastricht for a good reason. If currencies cannot stay together in the marketplace they are not ready to merge. If a country cannot control the amount it needs to borrow it will be a liability upon other countries that merge their monetary and borrowing policies with it. If countries are unwilling or reluctant to amend the statutes of their central banks to make them genuinely independent, it is a recognition of the democratic pressures that led to the establishment of a different system in the first place.

We should take heed. It is proving far too difficult to meet the Maastricht requirements. In the name of meeting those requirements the economies of Western Europe are suffering mightily. Budget cuts are being made at the wrong point in the economic cycle. Currency rates and interest rates have been too high for too long, further depressing economic activity. To pull out the democratic stabilizers at this point is the opposite of what is needed. People want lower interest rates, more sensible currency rates, more jobs and more economic growth; they are not desperate to transfer power to unelected central bankers whose only interest is the pursuit of zero inflation. The fact that this is not even a requirement of the statute of the German central bank and that Germany herself has never achieved zero inflation in the postwar period should serve as a warning to us all. It cannot work. It will throw Europe out of work rather than promoting prosperity.

PART 4
A EUROPE THAT WORKS

16

Renegotiation – the best course

At the turn of 1997 it became clear to many that Britain needed to renegotiate its deal in the European Community as a whole. The government over the preceding year had promised to renegotiate piecemeal several aspects: it was pledged to obtain a better deal for our fishermen; it said that it would work to obtain the lifting of the ban on beef exports; it said that it wished to see some changes in the procedures and powers of the European Court of Justice. It had made it clear that it did not wish to see major increases in the Community budget. It also had some reservations about the single-currency plan.

Many people felt that the European Community had moved too far away from the original idea of the Common Market. Instead of more trade, we were getting more government. Instead of furthering our prosperity, many of the regulations and economic policies were actively impeding economic progress. It was felt that the government should negotiate to get us back to something closer to the Common Market we had joined, further away from the European Union or European country that France and Germany were trying to create.

The single currency is crucial to any future renegotiation of our relationships with the partner economies of Western Europe. The single currency, as we have seen, is the single most important step on the federal road that any participating country could take. It is the crucial step away from a national economic policy towards a European one. It represents a substantial transfer of wealth and power from the national institutions to the European institutions. The question is 'Could Britain renegotiate a better deal in Europe without threatening withdrawal or being forced into withdrawal?'

There are many who say that the progress of the European union towards a country called Europe is inevitable. They believe that Britain has no influence over these events, unless Britain goes along with them. They see no future for Britain outside the European Community and no future for Britain as the difficult partner within it. Yet analysis of the position shows that if Britain wished to she could have an important, if not decisive, influence over the future direction of European Community policy.

At the moment there are two sets of negotiations under way in parallel on which Britain could bring decisive influence to bear. The first are the negotiations over the preparations for the single currency. The Community needs to legalize the euro and pass regulations accordingly. In the view of Germany and some others, it also needs to set up a Stability Pact, which again requires the voting support of the United Kingdom. There will be many other regulations coming before the Community to set up the institutions, procedures and practices for a single currency, some of which will require Britain's vote before they can go ahead. Whenever Britain has a power of veto she can have a decisive influence on the future shape of the Community, given the passion and strength of the Community's wish to move forward. Given the intensity of the French and German government's commitment to the single-currency scheme they would be prepared to make substantial concessions or amendments in order to secure Britain's vote to go ahead with these proposals.

Britain could also influence the proposals in the Inter-Governmental Conference. This Inter-Governmental Conference has a wide-ranging agenda for furthering the federal idea. France and Germany are proposing common foreign and security policies, substantial steps on the way to a common army and a common defence policy; common frontiers, with the abolition of frontier controls; more qualified majority voting to replace unanimous voting to decide issues within the Community. They want to strengthen the European Parliament, the Commission and the

Council of Ministers in various respects. Every one of these proposals requires Britain's active support and consent, as any treaty amendment has to be based on a unanimous vote of all member states.

Wielding the veto gives Britain substantial power. It is quite clear that Britain's view of a Europe of Nations is not compatible with a common foreign and defence policy, nor with more qualified majority voting, nor with strengthened powers for the Commission, the Parliament and the Council of Ministers. To have a proper Europe of Nations, we need a transfer of powers away from the European institutions back to member states' governments and more particularly back to companies, individuals and families – out of the hands of government altogether. We should, therefore, table our own agenda of genuine decentralization, deregulation, shedding of government power. We should demand this as our price for going along with any of the radical schemes that France and Germany favour for more integration between themselves. They want to use Community money and Community institutions for their plans.

Some say it is not feasible for Britain to carry on opting out of different parts of the Community's procedures. So far Britain has negotiated an opt-out from the Social Chapter, keeping more power to legislate over social and employment matters at home. We have also negotiated the right not to join the single currency, the most fundamental opt-out of them all. Britain has protected her right to keep her own borders and has said she will not cooperate with the scheme of common frontiers. Britain still has a veto over most matters of taxation, foreign policy and defence policy.

It is quite possible to construct a Community based upon flexible architecture. Those who wish the Community to take on a foreign and defence policy role have not yet suggested that Ireland, in order to remain a member of the Community will have to surrender her position of neutrality. Nor should they insist on this. If Ireland wishes to remain as a neutral country she should be able to do so, while still continuing to be a good member of the Community in every other respect. Similarly, if Britain wishes to keep her own economic policy separate from that of her partners but remain a member of the single market why should she not do so? When we first joined the Community in 1972 we made no promise that we would definitely abolish the pound and join a single-currency scheme at a later date. There would be no bad faith in Britain wishing to preserve her right to self-government in this important area.

The precedent of opt-out shows that it can be done. The criticism then turns to the proposition that we would not be able to negotiate further opt-outs because our partners are sick and tired of Britain following a lone course. Again, history does not bear out this criticism. Given that they need our vote to secure the radical changes they want, it would certainly be possible to negotiate an opt-out. If France and Germany are faced with the proposition that they cannot go ahead with their own defence- and foreign-policy merger unless Britain is given an opt-out from it then I am sure they will settle for giving Britain an opt-out.

Some suggest that it is not a right for Britain to delay progress towards a European state in this way. I would argue the opposite: that it is not fair that France and Germany constantly wish to use Community institutions for a purpose to which we never gave our consent. Nobody told us honestly when we joined the Community that we would be expected to pay the bills and to vote in support of the creation of a massive new government for Europe. Now that this is coming to pass it is not unreasonable for Britain to say that we do not wish to be part of those developments and we have no wish to pay the bills. If France and Germany wish to merge their economies, their foreign policy and their defence policy, that ultimately is a matter for them and their governments. If they wish to use our common institutions and have access to British taxpayers' money in order to do so, then Britain has every right to say 'No'.

Some say that using the veto to this considerable extent is tantamount to withdrawing from the European Community altogether. It is difficult to understand this argument. If somebody joins a cricket club and then discovers that some of the other members wish to change the rules to turn it into a rugby club as well, it would not be unreasonable for that person to oppose the change of rules. He could say that he wished his subscription to go only to the support of cricket and did not wish to have to pay a bigger subscription in order to cover the cost of rugby fixtures during the winter. The obvious answer would be for those wanting rugby as well to set up a separate rugby club. This is the position in which Britain finds herself *vis-à-vis* the European Community.

The European Community is a legal construct based on treaty, and interpretation of the treaty through the European Court. There is no clause or power in the treaty to expel a member of the Community. Whatever Britain did, the Community would be faced with the proposition that legally they could not remove us. There is certainly no power in the treaty or in natural law or natural justice that would enable the Community members to expel Britain because she had vetoed a number of proposals they supported. Nor would it be in the interests of Germany and France to try and get us out of the Community. Although they find it vexatious that we hold up a number of the changes they wish to see, they do find our £10,000m a year contribution extremely useful and they do want to trade with us as they sell us far more than we sell them. It is difficult to believe that Germany would say to us, 'Please do not buy our BMWs any more' or France, 'Please take the money away which you are currently giving to the poorer regions of France.' Both France and Germany know that it is in their trading and commercial interest to do business with Britain and both know that Britain is a fully paid up and legal member of the European Community.

The only option available to the French and Germans, if we did use the veto more than we currently do, would be to set up new institutions between themselves and any other states that wished to join. If they did this then they could do whatever they liked without needing our consent and without using our money. Of course France and Germany could have a common army and a common defence establishment if that is their wish; they would have to negotiate new arrangements with NATO but we would not be able to stop them.

What should Britain seek in the renegotiations?

Britain should set out a list of its requirements both for a more prosperous and successful Community as a whole and for happier relationships between Britain and the Community.

Britain's agenda for Europe should be an agenda to promote business and jobs. European government is getting in the way of prosperity. It is the high interest and exchange rates required by the Maastricht Treaty that have done so much damage to continental levels of employment. It is the laws and regulations from Brussels that are destroying the capacity of small businesses to expand and grow, to create the jobs that people need. Britain should set out an agenda based on flexible exchange rates, the end of the ERM, fewer rules and regulations, and markets more open to business success.

It is no accident that British levels of unemployment are now one third lower than the Community average and falling, whereas the Community average is still rising. Nor is it an accident that Asia and America have lower levels of unemployment than Britain. We must learn from their successes. Britain should propose deregulation of big industries like financial services, telecommunications and media, where many of the future jobs will lie. Britain should set out a list of two or three hundred directives that are no longer needed or that impede business success. The Community is in danger of stifling technical innovation. It does not need forty different directives specifying how you make different parts for a car in order to have a successful motor industry. Specifying too many things in legislation can make it illegal to improve or change products and components. Nor does it make sense to have such high levels of social protection for workers that companies are unable to employ extra employees, so that many millions of people stay on the dole.

Britain should insist that the principal aim of European policy should be the promotion of employment and prosperity. More than 18 million people are out of work in the European Community. That is more than the entire populations of Luxembourg, Ireland, Finland, Portugal and Greece put together. It is a sad testimony to political failure on a grand scale. The European Community now regularly meets and shakes its head about the problem and proposes small packages of measures based on the principle that you buy jobs by spending more public money. There is a double irony in this policy. Firstly, increasing Community spending means that more important programmes in domestic budgets have to be cut in order to meet the Maastricht convergence criteria. Secondly, it fails to understand that jobs come from a dynamic private-enterprise sector and not from recycling money through the public sector.

The United Kingdom should explain how a deregulated tele-communications and multi-media industry could be the centrepiece for massive economic growth and expansion in the next century. America has been much more successful than Western Europe here; by backing state monopolies, protective legislation and political intervention Europe has delivered less at much greater cost. CNN dominates world news-gathering. Hollywood dominates the world film industry. Ma Bell and her offshoots dominate the world telecommunications links. Only Britain, with a deregulated telecoms industry and the first signs of a deregulated media industry, is making some impact.

Britain's renegotiating aims over the single currency should be based on the proposition that either we must stop it or we must create a scheme which has more chance of working than the one currently on offer. The two go together, as any scheme with any chance of success will need fundamental treaty revision and this in turn will slow the whole process down and give time for France and Germany to think it all through in a more mature way. We should start from the proposition that you cannot have a currency union without a political union. Of course if a single currency is to work you need one central control over spending and tax levels as well as over borrowing. You need above all a single budget if you are to make sense of a single currency. You must have a single economic policy and there must be enough in common around the different parts of the currency union for a single interest rate and a single credit policy to have some chance of success. Convergence is everything. Britain must allow absolutely no fudging of the convergence requirements. They are the minimum preconditions. Indeed, Britain should say that they are not enough. We need to converge not just on interest rates, inflation rates and borrowing levels but also on employment levels, the flexibility of labour markets, productivity levels and all the other important things that go to create economic performance and success.

Britain should say a firm 'No' to the Stability Pact. It makes no sense whatsoever to fine a country 0.5 per cent of GNP when it is in difficulties. As we have seen, in 1992/3 this would have meant British taxpayers having to pay an extra 2 pence income tax as a fine to the European Community because the country was borrowing too much at the time, and more in subsequent years. The last thing an economy in recession needs is the imposition of a large fine, coupled with the requirement that taxes should be raised to pay it. The Stability Pact is no substitute for a single budget. Of course the borrowing of governments in the single-currency area must be strictly controlled. Better than imposing fines would be simply declaring the budget illegal and requiring the state to produce a new budget, accepting that political power had effectively been transferred to the monetary authorities for the union as a whole.

If Britain does not think these things through clearly, who will? The politicians gathered around the table from continental countries repeat that all that is required is another decisive move towards European union, without apparently understanding the terrible impact it could have on the lives, jobs and prosperity of millions of people in their countries. They are badly served by their advisers in the Community, who, with one or two notable exceptions, are not interested in pointing out the gross implausibilities and problems that lie ahead with the single-currency scheme of the Maastricht Treaty. It cannot work without proper political institutions to back it up. The European countries are not yet ready to be governed as one with a single economic policy. The interest rates that are right for Berlin under reconstruction will not be the same as those that are right for north-eastern France gripped by recession. The interest rates that are right for the technologically progressive Bavaria are not the same as those needed in south-western France with its rural economy. Nor would it be possible to go ahead without a huge increase in the transfer of monies around the different parts of the union. The level of transfers in the United States of America is six times that within the European Community and America enjoys the benefits of a single language and a flexible labour market. How much greater would the level of transfers need to be within the European Community to make any kind of sense at all?

Britain should talk with conviction about the dangers of a bodged currency union. She should use her veto to make Germany and France think it all through again; she should refuse to countenance the shift in the policy from the ecu of the treaty to the euro of the Regulation. She should refuse to accept the current Stability Pact. She should insist on treaty amendments that go to the heart of the issue, and the need to combine political and economic policy-making in one set of institutions.

And what should Britain demand for herself?

Britain should expect a far better deal for her fishermen. I was shocked when I visited Lowestoft to learn that a once great fishing port had fallen on extremely hard times. When we joined the European Community a hundred large British trawlers operated out of Lowestoft and plied a successful trade. Today there are just ten left. Under the current proposals from Commissioner Mrs Bonino another four vessels would have to disappear, leaving just 6 per cent of the fishing fleet the European Community inherited in 1972. On the day I visited, a normal working day, just one vessel came back to port with a catch. It took fifteen minutes to sell the fish in the fish market and that was the end of the day's work for all involved. When I asked where the other nine vessels were I was told that they could not fish that day because their quota did not entitle them to do so. Today many British vessels have to stay moored by the quayside and the fishermen watch as the Spanish and Dutch vessels come in and take the fish. If the Community will not give us a major increase in our quota, then Britain should reassert her 200-mile territorial limit. We could then reduce the total quota while massively increasing the quota that goes to the British fleet. Both conservation and the British industry would be well served by such a policy. What is stopping us?

Some say it would not be legal for Britain to reassert her 200-mile limits. All the legislation is in place, as the 200-mile limit currently operates for other resources of the deep. Aggregates dredged from the sea bed, oil, gas and similar natural assets are governed by a 200-mile or a median-point exclusion zone. All we would need to do is add fish into the relevant statute and regulations. Indeed, Mrs Bonino said that it lies in our own hands to settle the fishing industry. I presume this is what she had in mind.

However, threatening to do this would have such a big impact upon the Dutch and Spanish fishing industries that I am sure the European Community would soon want to talk about a better deal for Britain. We might well be able to negotiate a satisfactory increase in our quotas if we proposed as an alternative the reintroduction of our own territorial limits.

Some say that it would not be realistic to patrol the new territorial waters. Yet this is what we used to do before the common fisheries policy was introduced and that is exactly what countries like

Canada do against the interlopers from Spain. In the last Canadian/ Spanish fish war the British public were firmly on the side of the Canadians and many Canadian flags were seen flying in the ports and harbours of Britain to show solidarity for what the Canadians were doing. It could be done if we had the will to do it.

The European Court: servant or master?

The biggest problem we need to tackle is the power of the European Court of Justice. It is the European Court of Justice that is trying to undermine our opt-out from the Social Chapter. Their recent decision on the forty-eight-hour working-week directive has ruled that this particular piece of European legislation is governed by health and safety, which we do have to accept, and not by the Social Chapter, which we do not. The court is becoming a dangerous back door to force through a number of social and employment measures from which the government believed it had obtained exemptions. The European Court of Justice is the most federal of all the institutions. Its judges believe it is their role in life to push ever onward in a federal direction. They interpret the general preambles of the treaty in a generous way. They accept that the whole purpose of Community development is to create a country called Europe with an ever-bigger government from Brussels and Frankfurt.

Some say there is nothing we can do about the growing powers of the court. They say that we signed away our parliamentary supremacy when we joined the Community in 1972. They say that the court operates as a ratchet which will continue to turn against us and we must accept growing powers for the Community as adjudicated by the European Court. This is fatalism of the worst kind. What an Act of Parliament can grant it can take back. Our constitution is based upon two important propositions. The first is that an Act of Parliament is always sovereign. The second is that a parliament cannot bind its successors. Only an Act of Parliament can overturn an Act of Parliament. The whole purpose of democratic general elections is to decide which team of politicians the public would like to see legislating on their behalf. If a new team is elected it has the perfect right, subject to its manifesto and to public opinion, to change any Act of Parliament it inherits in the interests of the nation as it sees them.

This system has been gravely disrupted by the intrusion of the European Court of Justice. In practice a parliament has now bound its successors in an ever more restrictive way. The 1972 European Communities Act gives the European Court of Justice the power it needs to adjudicate cases affecting Britain. The European Court has moved from adjudicating cases to interpreting and making law. The court has decided it can overturn Acts of Parliament and Parliament so far has accepted this judgement. Unless Parliament challenges this principle soon then parliamentary democracy as we know it will have effectively been abolished. There will be an ever-growing range of issues which will not be settled by elected politicians in a free parliament but which have been or will be decided by a group of unelected judges in Europe. Already government ministers thinking of proposing legislation to the House of Commons have to ask first of all whether their legislation would be legal under European law. As European law expands it will become ever more important to know who makes European law and how it is made, and ever less important to win votes in the House of Commons. So what can be done to remedy this problem?

I would suggest a simple, one-clause Act of Parliament. This Act of Parliament would say that the European Court of Justice cannot overturn an Act of Parliament unless Parliament consents. The European Court of Justice should be able to advise, warn or urge that Britain amends its Acts of Parliament to bring them into line with the European Court's view of our treaty obligations. But if we wish to remain living in a parliamentary democracy ultimately Parliament must decide what our treaty obligations involve and how we wish to honour them. If Parliament decides that a government in good faith had opted us out of certain types of European legislation and if Parliament votes to reaffirm that, that should be the end of the matter. We should not have to accept European laws because the European Court has said it disagrees with our view of the treaty.

Some say that this would not work. The British courts might say that they believe that the European Court of Justice was supreme and that they would refuse to cooperate in implementing a law passed by Parliament which did not have the consent or agreement of the European Court of Justice as well. Our constitutional history used to be littered with disputes of this nature between the king, Parliament and courts in the sixteenth and seventeenth centuries. They were resolved then in favour of parliamentary supremacy. And so these disputes should be resolved today if such disputes still arise.

Some argue that if we took this view it would be tantamount to leaving the European Community. Again I disagree. Germany has done something similar already. The German Constitutional Court, in an important judgement, said that if a European Court ruling is in disagreement with the German constitution then ultimately the German constitution and the German parliament will prevail. If that is good enough for Germany, why can't something similar be good enough for Britain? To pass an Act of Parliament along the lines described would only bring us back to the position many people thought we were in when we joined the European Community in the first place.

Others say that the problem with doing this is that it would undermine the credibility of the European Court itself. They say that the European Court is more likely to be in our favour than against. They say that we need a strong European Court to ensure the fair and firm enforcement of common rules across the Community. What would happen, they say, to a British business needing access to the French market protected by European rules if the European Court was not there to enforce it against French jurisdiction?

While it is true that some British litigants do win cases in the European Court of Justice, it is also true to say that there have been a number of notable failures. The failure of the Community to take action against continental countries offering huge subsidies to their businesses to compete unfairly against British ones is worrying. The failure of the court to deal with all the restrictions to trade in a country like France is also flagrant. The use of the court in opening up the continental market to Britain has hitherto been distinctly limited.

We should propose in the Inter-Governmental Conference a new settlement for the court to try and avoid the need for unilateral action. We should try to get all countries to agree that their ultimate constitutional right must be to put through their own interpretation of the treaty. If you believe in a Europe of Nations that ultimately must be the position. There could be some new cases where this meant that a common rule was not properly enforced in a continental country against Britain's interests. It would also mean, however, that Britain could solve a number of its own big problems with the Community without any other legal trouble. We would gain much more than we lost.

For example, we could solve the problem of the beef ban on non-EC countries immediately if the supremacy of an Act of Parliament were restored. The beef ban has thrown many people out of work in the haulage business, the shipping and freight business, and the meat-processing business. It has cost British taxpayers around £3,500m in compensation as the British cattle herd is slaughtered on the altar of Brussels policy. Britain should be free to sell beef to willing buyers. Of course we have no automatic right to sell our beef to Germans, if Germans do not like our beef for one reason or another, whether that reason be well based or not. If we ruled that an Act of Parliament was sovereign again, then we could by Act of Parliament immediately lift the beef ban to non-EC countries. Britain does not believe it is in the EC jurisdiction anyway to ban beef sales to non-EC countries. If a South African wants to buy top-quality Scottish sirloin, why shouldn't he be free to do so without interference from the European Community? An Act of Parliament could lift the ban to non-EC countries immediately.

Similarly, restoring the sovereignty of an Act of Parliament would enable us to solve the fishing problem, allowing us to extend the 200-mile limit and median zone to cover fish.

Both these measures would create many more jobs. We would have bigger meat-processing and cattle-farming industries again, and much bigger fishing and fish-processing industries. Towns like Lowestoft, Grimsby and the Cornish fishing ports would come back to life.

Rather than having us pass such an Act of Parliament it is very likely the European Community would offer a compromise, limiting the power of the European Court of Justice to intervene in areas which we believe to be beyond its competence under the treaty. I am sure they would immediately be forthcoming with proper exemption on social and employment matters to back up the exemption we thought we had secured at Maastricht. They might well throw in proper protection over borders and frontiers, which is the next area they are likely to move in on, and a better deal on beef and fish.

All this shows that constructive negotiating progress could be made if we combined carrot and stick. The carrot must be twofold. We must always consider compromise when they start to meet our needs and we should offer them the prospect of our allowing their federal progress. The stick must be to have in mind a series of measures which could solve the problem by direct and unilateral action if the Community fails to give us what we need.

The big issue is whether Britain can save Europe from itself. Europe is falling further and further behind fast growth rates of Asia. It is falling behind because government is too big and expensive, and there are too many laws and regulations being passed. The single currency would make the problem much worse if it went ahead on the basis of the treaty. It is Britain's duty to warn our partners before it is too late and to block the important parts of the scheme to protect the jobs and livelihoods of those who will otherwise suffer from these proposals.

The European Community is now spending a lot of our money on propaganda to persuade people that the single currency would be good for them and their jobs. The protagonists tell us that it would mean lower interest rates, more trade and more economic activity. There is not a shred of evidence to support these contentions. The dry run for the scheme, the ERM, ended in ignominious failure, with much higher unemployment and a great deal of unnecessary business loss. French and German long-term real interest rates have been higher for fifteen years than those in Britain, and yet we are told that by joining France and Germany we will have lower real long-term interest rates than we have been enjoying over that period. Britain's message must be that the way to get more jobs in Europe is to cast aside the Maastricht single-currency scheme, not to reinforce it. We should all take a deep breath, sit down and think again. We should think through the consequences of going ahead with the currency union when the economies are not in line with one another. Above all, we should warn that a currency union without a political union would be a very troublesome birth of a very unhealthy infant.

17

A more prosperous Europe without the euro

Christopher Johnson, in his Penguin, *In with the Euro, Out with the Pound: The Single Currency for Britain*, claims to have dismissed dangerous illusions about European Economic and Monetary Union. He states that EMU is likely to happen. He is right that the French and German governments are totally committed to it and seem prepared to inflict enormous pain on their electorates in pursuit of this will-o'-the-wisp. He is wrong to assume from this that there is an inevitability about the single currency. The scheme is riddled with inconsistencies and dangers and is not attracting much popular support from electorates around Western Europe. Britain, if she wished, could have a decisive influence. Britain has the power to block the legalization of the euro and the Stability Pact, and could use her bargaining position to derail the system. It should do so in the interests of jobs and prosperity across Europe.

Johnson argues that it is vital to have a timetable. He is right in that a timetable helps to concentrate minds; it is part of the process by which French, German and other sympathetic governments are trying to bamboozle the rest of us into joining the single currency. The artificial timetable they have created has slipped once already, but it is now driving the process forward. It is only vital to have a timetable if you believe it is vital to go into monetary union. For all those who are against monetary union or who believe that the economies of Western Europe are not ready for it, it is equally vital to insist that there should be a pause for thought, to see if economies can genuinely converge.

Johnson believes it will do immense harm to wait and see. He

believes Britain should say now that we will be in the first group
going ahead to monetary union in 1999. His reasons, that Britain
outside the first group of countries would have a lower exchange
rate, a lower economic growth rate and higher interest rates than
if she was in, are difficult to sustain in serious argument. Britain
outside the ERM and undecided about entry is experiencing at the
moment a strengthening of her currency. Britain will only have
higher interest rates than the other partners if, at the point of their
entry into the single currency, the British economy is booming
and needs higher interest rates to curb inflationary pressures. If
the cycle is the other way round and the British economy is in
decline, then of course Britain will have lower interest rates and
will need lower interest rates than the continental countries in
order to cushion the recession. There is no reason to suppose that
the UK will have to devalue or depreciate the pound if Britain
stays out of the currency union. Britain could, if she wished and
judged it right, have a stronger currency than the euro. To do so
she would obviously need a tougher counter-inflation policy than
the euro area and might well need higher interest rates. Alternatively she might choose a different mixture of policy advantages,
which could include lower interest rates and the pound stable or
even depreciating against the euro, taking into account whether
the pound was at the same time rising or falling against the dollar
and the yen.

Johnson argues that Britain does not need to become more
competitive before joining, assuming, wrongly, that the over-
valuation of the pound in the ERM was corrected when we left it.
He speaks as if rates, costs and prices do not move on. The whole
point about exchange rates and price levels is that they are infinitely
variable depending on the individual circumstances of countries,
companies and economies. When he was writing his book the
pound may well have been very competitive against the Deutschmark and the French franc. Today, as I write this, people are
worried that the pound is again overvalued against the continental
currencies following a period of sterling strength. There is no right

rate to enter the ERM and certainly no right rate at which you could enter a single currency.

Johnson believes we would be worse off outside the single currency. Turning on its head the usual argument that we do so much business with the continent of Europe we must therefore join our currency with theirs, he points out that the City of London does far more business with the rest of the world than with Europe. He uses this to deduce that there is substantial unrealized potential which the City could exploit once Britain had joined the single currency. The contrary is nearer the truth. The City of London needs to remain offshore from the euro area whether Britain has joined it or not. The City of London relies upon running big dollar and yen businesses and other markets, and relies upon free movements of capital around the world. It would not flourish under Frankfurt-style banking controls. Johnson believes that we have little freedom of monetary policy at the moment. This is based on the unwarranted assumption that we wish to keep the pound stable against the Deutschmark and that this determines our monetary policy. As I have shown, when we did this we lost our freedom for manoeuvre and we ripped out the stabilizers that would otherwise have cushioned the United Kingdom economy. Now that we are no longer trying to keep the pound in line with the Deutschmark, we have considerable freedom of monetary policy. If Germany increases or reduces her interest rates tomorrow there is no need for Britain to follow suit, though we would have to follow suit if we were worried about the consequences of the German move for the Anglo-German exchange rate.

The most breathtaking assertion of all is that the single market needs a single currency. Johnson draws a distinction between a single market and a free-trade area. There is no reason to single out currency fluctuations amongst all the differences and divergences which exist between the different European economies. Could it not equally well be argued that you cannot have a proper single market unless the tax levels in each country are identical? That you would have to harmonize the labour laws and make sure that social and pension costs were similar around the Community? That there would have to be deliberate policies to bring productivity, education and training into line around the Community to have a so-called fair single market?

The theory of international trade is based upon the theory that different countries and companies have different advantages which they should reinforce. International trade requires specialization and it requires an admission on the part of the trading partners that one country is favoured in one way and others in another. There is no reason why other Community countries should have a share of our oil, any more than there would be any justice in saying that because the Mediterranean countries have a better climate, enabling them to grow citrus fruits and olives, we ought to have a share of their citrus and olive crops. We should welcome the fact that different levels of educational achievement, different climates, different skills in the workforce, different levels of costs and different exchange rates add to the variety of the international market-place.

Johnson asserts that ordinary people will accept the monetary union. He admits that it will require a huge popular education campaign if the euro is to be introduced successfully and if a referendum is to be won. He stretches credulity a little by saying that as many as a third to a half of British people currently support the single currency. The *Sun*'s poll showed that only 1 in 20 supported the single currency; the more general opinion polls suggest that support is well below one fifth of the electorate. People are naturally suspicious of the single currency. They realize that it is the transfer of more than coinage, a huge transfer of sovereignty from Britain to the continent.

Johnson believes that the single currency need not divide Europe. He believes that twelve of the fifteen countries will be ready in 1999 if Britain and Denmark relent and decide to join. He states, 'A single currency is not a suitable subject for variable geometry, so that it does not matter who chooses to join and who would not. It is an integral part of European union and the monetary component of economic and monetary union.' In other words Johnson agrees that if the UK and Denmark remain outside, along with some countries who cannot meet the convergence criteria, the single-currency scheme will split Europe. On his own analysis, even if Britain agreed to go in, the single-currency area would still split Europe. Not only would it leave outside a minority of European Union countries but it would continue to exclude all the non-EU countries, both rich and poor, on our borders. There is no suggestion that Norway and Switzerland or the Czech Republic, Hungary and Poland are going to join. Johnson, along with other advocates of European union, misunderstands the geographical realities of Europe. Europe does not stop at the East German border or at the Swiss frontier. The more that the European Union or a group of its states integrate with each other, the more they split Europe as a whole.

Johnson's ninth point is that 'it will make enlargement meaning-ful'. Belatedly recognizing the danger of a split Europe, he then takes a wider view and argues that although the excluded states to the east cannot join the European Union before monetary union has taken place, they should be forced to make rapid progress to meet the convergence requirements so that they could in due course take their place within the single currency. This is wishful thinking on a grand scale. The economies of Eastern Europe are so different from the economies of Germany or France that there is no realistic prospect of them converging with the Franco-German economy in the foreseeable future.

Johnson concludes that the single currency would not mean the end of the nation state. He concedes: 'Political union of a limited kind is needed to persuade Germany to give up the Deutschmark, and to make the European Union work better.' He then, however, perpetuates the myth that there would not need to be increased transfer payments around the union, there would be no need for common taxation and no single economic policy. This is simply unrealistic. Of course there will have to be much stronger moves to political union if the single currency is to have any chance of success.

There is a positive case to be made out for keeping the pound. The question of what is an optimum area for a currency union is a difficult one. Twenty years ago Ireland decided that the sterling currency union was too large and set up a separate currency. In the late 1980s Scottish nationalists felt they would like to do something similar. These are matters of national identity.

The example of the United States of America shows that large currency unions can be very successful. It is true that the United States of America has achieved dramatic growth and prosperity in the twentieth century as a currency union. It is also true that the United States of America achieved an even more phenomenal economic development in the nineteenth century, when it was not a currency union. The creation of the dollar as the American single currency was an important part of the expression of nationhood of the American peoples. It has caused considerable economic difficulties in some parts of the American union. These have had to be offset as best they can by subsidies and transfer payments.

Britain has a lot to be proud of in the last twenty years. She has achieved a higher rate of growth than her European partners. She has tackled many of the difficulties of burgeoning public-sector budgets and welfare spending before her continental partners. By deregulation and free-enterprise policies she has created considerable strength for herself in new areas like multi-media, telecommunications, business services, financial services, legal services and pharmaceuticals. All of these industries sell around the world. They are particularly strong in selling in English-speaking territories. While Britain exports capital around the world she is particularly keen on exporting capital to the large American market where a common language and culture make investment and business activity easier.

Britain should keep the pound and think globally. The future lies in the global market using the English language and mobilizing talent and capital through the City of London and through companies large and small founded in or operating from a United Kingdom base.

Britain could warn Europe before it is too late that single currencies without political unions cannot work, that we need a common market but not a common government, and that over-regulation will damage the competitiveness of Western Europe.

The more different aspects of the single-currency scheme are revealed to the British people, the more worried they become. There was a sense of shock when the public first recognized that our gold and convertible currency reserves would be transferred to Frankfurt and would no longer necessarily be used on our behalf at our request. There was another sense of injustice, when it emerged that one way or another the unfunded pension liabilities in France and Germany would come back to haunt us if we were to join a currency union with them. In 1996 people saw the impact of common policies on our fishing industry and our beef industry all too vividly. They began to ask themselves whether they could really trust economic and monetary policy to the institutions that were wreaking such havoc in our agricultural and marine industries.

Keep the pound and keep your country. The abolition of the pound is not a mere technical matter for bankers: it goes to the heart of parliamentary democracy. Once a country has joined a single currency controlled by a distant independent central bank, there is no point in discussing many of the important matters of economic policy in general elections or in parliamentary debate. There would be nothing that British politicians could do if your business was unable to obtain credit, if your house price was plummeting because interest rates were too high, if you were unable to export to America or Japan because the level of the euro had soared against those currencies or if taxes went up to pay for the resulting mess in the currency union. The single currency is a massive step on the road to the creation of a country called Europe. It is being created by technocrats. Its power will be operated behind closed doors without proper democratic debate. The record of the technocrats so far is lamentable. Their ERM blew up in their hands. It did untold damage to millions of families, depressing their house prices, destroying many jobs and throwing many businesses into bankruptcy. Now the technicians tell us that they should be trusted with ultimate power in a bank in Frankfurt. They tell us that the ERM did not work, not because it was flawed in concept, but because their powers did not go far enough in controlling and directing our lives.

Britain must use her vote to veto the scheme as it stands, pointing out that consent is needed for government. Many countries of Western Europe already have problems with consent within their own borders: it will not create a happier Europe to impose a more remote central authority from Brussels. Far from assuaging regional and local feelings, it will serve to inflame them further.

The concept of European union died with the collapse of the Holy Roman Empire. It died on the fields of Flanders and in the streets of Berlin in 1945. It should not be revived by peaceful means. The Western European peoples are better off living in peace one with another, organizing their governments at a more local level than Brussels. To force union upon them in the face of their marked reluctance to accept it can but lead to disaster.